CANADA

IN THE NINETIES:

Meltdown or Renaissance ?

iv

Published by
World Media Institute Inc.
549 Besserer Street,
OTTAWA, Canada, K1N 6C6   FAX: (613) 238-5249
and

The Gamma Institute Press Ltd.,
3636 avenue Du Musée,
Montreal, Quebec,
Canada, H3G 2C9

Cover design by Studio M Saucier Inc., Montreal
Final edit/make-up/page layout/typesetting using Quark XPress and
Macintosh SE by Jane Stuart APR
Linotronic Services by ARTEXT Electronic Publishing Inc.

Printed by
Trigraphic Printing (Ottawa) Limited
485 Industrial Avenue,
OTTAWA, Canada K1G 0Z1

Canadian Cataloguing-in-Publication Data

Valaskakis, Kimon, 1941 -
  Canada in the Nineties

Includes bibliographical references.
ISBN   0-921957-02-5

  1. National characteristics, Canadian. 2.Canada - Economic policy.
3. Nationalism - Canada. 4. Canada - Politics and government.
I. World Media Institute. II. Groupe des Associés Montréal-McGill
pour l'étude de l'Avenir (GAMMA). III. Title.

FC.V34 1990   971   C90-090107-1
F1008.3.V34 1990

Ce livre est disponible en français sous le titre "Le Canada dans les années 90:
effondrement ou renaissance?"

CANADA
IN THE NINETIES:
Meltdown or Renaissance ?

by
Kimon Valaskakis

DEDICATION

to
my father, Platon,
and my mother, Marie-Claire,
in recognition
of much more than the gift of life.

CONTENTS

x

CANADA IN THE NINETIES
Meltdown or Renaissance ?
by Kimon Valaskakis,

ISBN   0-921957-02-5

other titles by the author:

Economic Nationalism and French Trade 1870-1914
Le Québec et son destin international
The Conserver Society   (with Peter S. Sindell, J.G.Smith,
E.I.Fitzpatrick-Martin)
La Société de conservation   (with Peter S. Sindell, J.G.Smith,
E.I.Fitzpatrick-Martin)
Le futur du Québec au conditionnel   (with R. Jouandet-Bernadat,
P Fréchette, R. Blais, P. Dansereau)
Prospective de la langue française au Québec   (with others)

ACKNOWLEDGEMENTS

The publication of this book coincides with the dawn of the nineties and the launching of the ISOGroup International Network, a Montreal-based global consulting and planning network.

The two events are inter-related. ISO stands for 'Intelligence', 'Strategy' and 'Organization', the three ingredients needed to face rapid social change. As events in Eastern Europe and elsewhere indicate, time is not standing still. We are entering a period of major turbulence most of which, hopefully, will be creative and positive, but by no means straightforward.

To cope successfully with these challenges, private-sector firms, government departments, international agencies and even individuals need good 'intelligence' of how major socio-economic trends will affect them, a coherent 'strategy' on how to extract the opportunities and to avoid the threats generated by these trends, and a good 'organization' to implement the chosen strategy.

ISO, then, is an antidote to complexity and to what Alvin Toffler has aptly called "future shock". If the approach is meaningful at the level of individuals, firms and government agencies, it is even more necessary at the level of a nation such as Canada. Hence, this book is an attempt to effect a major 'strategic rethink' of the nation in this last decade of the twentieth century.

I would like to express my thanks to, and acknowledge the help of a number of people who have contributed to the publication of this book.

First, I wish to recognize the financial support offered by the National Capital Commission and its chairperson, Mrs. Jean Piggott, and by my ISOGroup colleagues David Amar, Robert Coull, Samir Chakour and Raoul Elias.

Second, I offer special thanks for the intellectual inputs of Christian de Laet, Robert Clermont, Stephane Gendron and Yianis Philopoulos of the Gamma Institute, Raoul Elias of Pragma, Leonard Dudley, my colleague at the Economics Department of the University of Montreal, and Ron Desroches and Pierre Allard of the National Capital Commission. I am also grateful for the comments of Peter White, formerly of the Prime Minister's Office, and Norman Spector of the Privy Council Office.

Third, I thank my copy editors, Sharon Gubbay Helfer and Jane Stuart, for their patient and painstaking help.

Finally, I thank my immediate family and friends for their support and encouragement during the long 'incubation' period during which this book was 'hatched'.

KIMON VALASKAKIS
Montreal,
January 6th, 1990

FOREWORD

Every Canadian patriot will be challenged by reading "Canada in the Nineties". Everyone concerned for the future of the world who believes Canada could play a vital role in shaping global society during the next century, even in this decade, should read this book.

The ideas expressed herein are intended to inform, illuminate and stimulate the discussion and debate concerning Canada's immediate future, and to motivate those who are concerned by the potential 'meltdown' of our nationalism. If we are to have a renaissance, it must grow out of our frustrated anxiety into informed concern and become relevant involvement in creating a 'magnificent destiny' for Canada.

Our tomorrow is being shaped by today's decisions. Canadians are, therefore, now determining their nation's future by deciding whether Canada, as they know it, is worth preserving. By our individual actions, by our personal priorities, lifestyles and commitments, during this decade, **we** are determining whether this nation survives as Canada, a community that has nurtured us and, for many, given us our cultural identity.

Do **you** believe Canada will exist, as such, by the year 2,000? Will we be **ready**, and as citizens of an enlightened and powerful nation, **willing** and **able** to be a relevant and dynamic force for creative change in the world of the 21st Century?

Or will we be self-seeking, security-minded survivalists, concerned only with the prosperity of ourselves and our province, our race, our religion or our language group? Will humanity have been sacrificed to the god of our private goals and our unwillingness to think and stretch beyond ourselves?

This is what Kimon Valaskakis lays before us, personally, corporately and politically, as a series of choices, challenges and consequences. As Canadians, we have, indeed, 'choices to make, premises to keep and kilometres to go before we sleep!'

For Valaskakis, it is truly 'Meltdown or Renaissance for Canada in the Nineties' and, he makes clear, those choices rest with ordinary citizens, not their political leaders alone.   For if the task of democratic leaders is to **reflect** their citizens beliefs, not to **direct** them, then each of us must examine the kind of Canada we want, and consider what the world needs from us in this decade, and beyond.

America was first to reach the moon by conceptualizing itself as being there, and then figuring out how to get home! Perhaps Canadians should be first to think of themselves as citizens of the planet, and then work back to the kind of national and local communities which will be needed, if the world is to survive and life is to be sustained in this global, human community.

Wherever we begin, it is timely to consider 'Canada in the nineties - meltdown or renaissance?' as the choice each of us is making, by neglect and default, or by care and concern, in the next few months and years.

Whether we will be singing "Oh Canada" as this decade ends, may depend on how many of us respond to the challenge of "Canada in the Nineties: Meltdown or Renaissance?". We will have to decide if this nation, in some familiar form, needs and deserves our commitment and active support.

By doing so, we can avoid far more radical changes and uncomfortable circumstances for ourselves and our families in the next decade. If we earnestly seek, in this decade, the changes which are needed - starting with ourselves - a new Canada will emerge by the year 2,000.

WAYNE KINES
World Media Institute,
Ottawa, January, 1990

INTRODUCTION

The Prospect for Excellence
and the Spectre of Mediocrity

Canada and Argentina were singled out at the
beginning of this century by many analysts as the leading
future superpowers. As the twentieth century is coming to
a close, Argentina has clearly not fulfilled its promise. It is
still racked by internal tensions, a troubled political past
and a weak economy.

But what about Canada? As the nineties unfold,
Canada appears to be superbly-endowed by nature and
circumstance to perform very well in the world economy.
The potential for excellence is certainly there and Canada's
image abroad has been strikingly positive. In one recent
survey, a number of respondents in Europe and Asia were
asked to list which country they would prefer living in after
their own. An overwhelming majority mentioned Canada.
There is no doubt that both the natural and the human
resources for superlative performance are available in
plentiful supply. However, accompanying the promise of
superlative performance there is also a major spectre of
mediocrity.

In fact, in some strange masochistic sense, the
country seems to condemn itself to this mediocrity by
refusing to deal adequately with some major structural
issues that have dogged it throughout its history. These
issues now crystallize around two major challenges, an
external and an internal one.

The external one has to do with Canada's
relationship with its only neighbour, the United States - a
relationship which has, over the years, gone through all the

steps of a 'hesitation waltz' or a Latin American cha-cha: one step forward, two backwards, three to the side. The approach-avoidance mode which has characterized this relationship is likely to come to a head in post-free-trade North America. A full scale of integration options, including political integration, are likely to surface in the nineties. Two forces are at work in the world economy: globalization and continentalism. As we will show later, the more powerful force, as far as Canada is concerned, is now continentalism, edging Canada closer to the Manifest Destiny which, in nineteenth-century North America was considered inevitable.

The external challenge is augmented by an internal one. It relates to Canada's inability to balance successfully the centrifugal forces pulling the country apart with the centralizing forces keeping it together. The wild swings back and forth have spawned what I have called, "Canada's National Adversary System". At least four major adversary systems make up the body politic, supplemented by a host of minor ones, themselves fuelled by an adversarial mind-set. The question that arises is the following : *Can Canada afford these adversary systems in the face of rising continental integration or is it signing itself off by doing that?* Is Canada set on a meltdown process with eventual absorption by the United States as the necessary outcome, or can it create a new modus vivendi?

Even if the penalty of the adversarial mode is not cancellation of the country, it may nevertheless be heavy. The primary thesis of this book is that the adversarial philosophy stymies initiative and locks entrepreneurs out of the full cycle of innovation. Good ideas cannot come to fruition in the country and must go elsewhere to be developed. We end up exporting ideas and creative thinkers and re-importing the products that these ideas have created.

To paraphrase a saying, an increasing number of products may well read, "invented in Canada, patented in the United States and ... made in Japan!" This situation confirms the basic Canadian paradox: an immense potential for excellence and a sub-optimal performance - not a bad performance, mind you, but a middling one.

Depending on how the two challenges are met - and they must be met in consistent fashion - the nineties are likely to be characterized by one of four scenarios. In the first, the pattern of 'muddling through', that presently characterizes the country's behaviour, continues. The immense endowment of the country allows it to move along, not smartly but painfully, into the twenty-first century and beyond, a good but uninspiring performance in various fields. The gentleman's 'C' is the rule and superlatives go elsewhere. By continuing to muddle through, Canada condemns itself to mediocrity.

In the second scenario, the deterioration of the body politic splits the country apart, with Quebec leaving Confederation. This is the 'Meltdown Version 1'. It is followed by the merger of English Canada with the United States. Quebec initially remains apart, but then joins the rest of North America with a special status, somewhere between Puerto-Rico and Louisiana.

With the third scenario, a second version of the 'Meltdown' occurs. Canada drifts apart, Quebec separates, English Canada joins the United States but Quebec remains separate and strengthens links with the European Community. This scenario is a very long-shot but not completely impossible.

In the fourth scenario, the 'Meltdown' is avoided altogether and a Canadian 'Renaissance' occurs. A new 'mission statement' is achieved, closer to what is known in French as a *projet de société*. National energies are harnessed and focused to realize it. The adversarial systems are replaced by the search for synergy, goal congruence and team work. As a result, the country not only survives but thrives and optimizes the generous bounty with which nature has endowed it.

The dateline for these events is the decade of the nineties. Although it is conceivable that other scenarios may occur or that things may actually not come to a head before the year 2000, it is probable that for Canada the *rendez-vous with history* will occur in this decade. The combined forces of Free Trade, Globalization and Constitutional Reform (the Meech Lake Accord) are likely to force a showdown before the nineties come to a close.

Intellectual Roots

Why was this book written? It was conceived twenty-two years ago when I arrived as an immigrant to Canada from the United States after having studied and lived in a number of other countries. Born in Egypt of Greek parents, my peregrinations had taken me successively to France, Britain and then the United States. Canada was then, in my private perception, a speck among others in a crowded universe and my first appreciation of it came with distinctly American-conditioned eyes. This was the year of Expo 67, the time when Montreal was establishing itself on the world map. Fresh out of graduate school at Cornell University, I sought in Canada a temporary sojourn - a couple of years to soak in the Paris of North America, then back to some university in

California where my real career would start. But Montreal engaged my emotions as well as my curiosity, and the place that was supposed to provide a brief interlude after the gruelling years of writing the PhD thesis, became the locus of long-term settlement. From that time, at the back of my mind, between teaching, international assignments, the founding of the Gamma Institute, and various consultancies, lurked fundamental questions as to the nature of this addictive, yet strangely ambivalent, country. Slowly but surely the book incubated.

Let me reassure the reader that the actual writing of the book did not take twenty-two years. With the marvels of modern convivial computers, the drafting was relatively painless and occurred principally in the second half of 1988.

My first attempt at understanding Canada and writing about it came in 1980 when, in the throes of the great Quebec Referendum Debate, I wrote a book on the probable consequences of Quebec independence. This book, entitled *Le Québec et son destin international*, examined three variants of Quebec independence: a purely symbolic independence with little substance, an 'autonomist' limited self-rule, and a full-fledged true independence. The book's thesis was essentially a paraphrasing of Einstein's famous dictum on the relationship between geometry and experience. In the Quebec-Canada context it claimed that "insofar as independence was real it was not feasible and insofar as it was feasible ... it was not real". The book was the end result of a major three-year project undertaken first for the Bourassa and then the Lévesque administrations on the future of Quebec. One of its by-products was to emphasize the need to understand Canada better given the close relationship between "what Quebec wants" and "what Canada does not want".

In 1983-1984, the Gamma Institute was given a mandate by the National Capital Commission (NCC) in Ottawa, to examine ways and means of enhancing the role of the Ottawa-Hull Region, not just as another urban agglomeration, but as the true national capital of Canada.

Since a capital is supposed to reflect its country intimately, for every vision of Canada there could be one or more corresponding visions of the capital. If Canada were viewed as a strongly centralized federation, then a Washington-type capital, complete with an independent federal district, would be called for. If, on the other hand, Canada were to be regarded as a very loose confederation, a community of communities, a mosaic of distinct societies, then a Berne-type capital would be more appropriate. Berne is the capital of the highly successful Swiss Confederation. It is not glamorous, not an international city, but essentially nice and quiet, clean, green, efficient and quite beautiful. The Swiss government is a sort of a holding company where major orientations are chosen, but the real power lies with the cantons.

Between Washington and Berne is a long continuum of intermediate possibilities, but it was clear that only by clearly defining Canada could the role of the capital be properly determined. Part of the strategic planning of the National Capital Region was, then, the need to examine where Canada itself was going. Consequently, in the process of completing this consulting project, we had occasion to deepen our understanding of Canada. In 1987, a few years after the report to the NCC was submitted under the title *Ottawa-Hull, a Capital in Search of a Role*, I decided to put on paper a book on

Canada, partially based on that project. The chairperson of the NCC, Mrs. Jean Piggott, was kind enough to offer financial support towards the endeavour, for which I must acknowledge a sincere debt of gratitude. The encouragement offered both by Mrs. Piggott and by the staff of the NCC was very stimulating and helpful in bringing this project to fruition.

This being said, the usual caveats must be stated: the book reflects only my personal views and engages no one else's responsibility, either at the NCC or at the Gamma Institute. In addition it should be clearly stated that this is meant as a non-partisan essay on the future of Canada. Both the greatness and the shortcomings of this country are attributable to all parties and the avenues of solution not fundamentally incompatible with any of the three major political groupings - from right to left, the Conservatives, the Liberals and the New Democrats. Although each one of us has political leanings and preferences, nation-building must be a notch above partisan pettiness. Every citizen must be politically committed - Pericles used to say in the Athenian agora that those citizens who were not interested in politics not only had no business there, but probably had no business at all. However, there are national-level questions which, by their very nature, must be multi-partisan.

Seed-Events

The actual forces which are likely to shape the nineties reached a point of accumulation in October 1987 and further strengthened my resolve to write this book. "There is a tide in the affairs of men which taken at the flood leads on to fortune / Omitted all the voyage of their life is bound in shallows and in miseries ..." So spoke

Cassius in Shakespeare's play. The month of October 1987 was one such tide. By an unusual confluence of circumstances, a number of major streams likely to affect deeply the future of Canada dominated the headlines. Each of these, taken singly, appeared as a routine topical issue - alongside accidents, burglaries and the daily weather. Taken in combination, however, they collectively constitute what futurists like to call *seed-events* - individual occurrences which carry within them the potential for sweeping change, for better or for worse. A thorough and early appraisal of such seed-events is essential in order to avoid *strategic surprise* - the condition that occurs when we are assailed by a future which descends upon us suddenly and without warning.

There were at least five such seed-events in the fateful month of October 1987. One was of global proportions: the stock market crash of October 19. The crash was the worst single-day fall of the Dow Jones in history, and may have long-term implications which will become evident years from now. October 29, 1929 saw the Dow lose 12 percent of its value. October 19, 1987 saw it fall by 22 percent. The whole pattern of the decade that followed the 1929 crash was conditioned by it and by the attempts by governments to respond to it. Will the same occur in the nineties or will the 1987 crash be a mere passing aberration, a market correction of no consequence? Either way the events leading up to and immediately following the crash revealed significant changes in the world economy full of portent and potential. Perhaps the most significant was the growing importance of Japan and the Asian capital markets in today's global economy.

The three other major seed-events were of North American importance. The first two are obvious and are destined to crowd the headlines for a long time to come: the *Meech Lake Constitutional Accord* was signed in early October by a majority of provinces and the *Free Trade Agreement* negotiated in its penultimate form at the end of that month. The philosophy behind Meech Lake is to transfer power from the federal government to the provinces and the philosophy behind free trade is to transfer power from all governments to the free market.

What could result from both is a smaller, less powerful federal government. In 1985, the proportion of what we call the 'public sector' in Canada still controlled by the federal government, was about 45 percent, with the rest belonging to provincial, municipal and other levels. By the end of the century, with opting-out by provinces from federal programmes, the central government's spending power might fall to the 20 percent level. If this happens, it will mean that the principal instruments of public sector intervention will no longer be in the hands of one governing body but will be increasingly diffuse and decentralized. Will this result in a highly decentralized confederation with the Canadian federal government as the holding company?

For all the perplexities that a post-Meech Lake Canada may raise, it appeared, at the time of writing, to be devoutly-wished by Quebec. A permanent rejection of the Meech Lake Accord or of close alternatives, may give rise to a new momentum for Quebec nationalism, a vital movement which has historically alternated between latency and great dynamism. The resurgence of this nationalism may, in turn, trigger ricochet movements elsewhere in the land with combinatorial effects of great significance. For instance, strong Quebec nationalism in the nineties may feed Western separatism and Maritime

discontent. Will Quebec nationalism enter a new radical
phase in the nineties? Will the economic link with the
United States lead Québécois into reassessing their
membership in Canada? Or will the increasing pressures
of continentalism create a new national unity in Canada ?

A fifth seed-event of 1987 was *tax reform* in both
the United States and Canada. The U.S. tax reform
appears more substantive than the Canadian, since there is
a suspicion here that what governments give with one hand
they take away with the other. Nevertheless, both tax
reforms spring from the same basic ideology, one that
gathered momentum in the early eighties: minimizing
government's role in the economy, cutting it down to size,
reducing its gluttony. Will the goal of state minimization
be successful, or will the changes remain superficial? In
particular, given free trade, will Canada be able to afford a
more severe tax system than that of the United States,
without risking a brain drain of skilled professionals
seeking a more affluent life south of the border?
Conversely, given free trade can Canada afford not to have
a well-funded government to discharge its mounting
responsibilities?

There are two interesting characteristics of the
seed-events of the autumn of 1987. The first is that every
one of them uncovered a basic set of problems not born in
1987, but having deep historical roots. The second is that
the events, when taken in combination, yield effects and
permutations that are not immediately obvious when they
are considered singly. This combinatorial dimension has
largely been ignored by the media and the politicians who
have instead focused their attention on each separately, not
looking at the all-important linkages. The seed-events of
October 1987 found fuller fruition at the end of 1988. On

November 21 1988, Canada re-elected a Conservative majority with an implicit mandate to go ahead with the Free Trade Agreement with the United States. Consequently, the Agreement came into operation in January 1989 and the ten-year countdown for its completion began. In December 1988, the Supreme Court of Canada struck down some of the provisions of Bill 101 in Quebec. Given the strong sentiments that Quebec nationalism engendered and the surge of linguistic tensions in that province, Premier Bourassa chose a compromise solution, Bill 178, that managed to antagonize both Anglophones and Francophones. In addition, the Quebec government used for the first time the so-called 'notwithstanding clause', a provision built into the Canadian Constitution that, in effect, cancels the Charter of Rights and Freedoms whenever provincial governments choose to do so.

Emerging Issues

Canada enters the nineties, then, with a number of question-marks. The first is connected with the Free Trade Agreement. How far will free trade go? As the new decade unfolds and we near the end of the millennium, will the Agreement really turn-out to be 'just a commercial deal' or will it blossom into full-fledged integration of the two countries. Will 'creeping continentalism', a feature that has dominated Canada's history since the beginning of the nineteenth century, become 'galloping continentalism'? Will Canada, some time, some day, spurred by the example of European integration, decide to cast its lot with its southern neighbour?

The second question mark relates to the future of Confederation. Can a decentralized, diffuse Canada coexist in equal partnership with the strongest federation on earth, or will internal centrifugal forces coalesce with continentalism to accelerate and render inevitable what the nineteenth-century Americans were calling Manifest Destiny?

In this sense, there is an apparent dilemma. From Quebec's viewpoint, at least as expressed in the November 21, 1988 federal election, the weakening of Canada is seen as the strengthening of Quebec. A number of Quebec voters argued then that if the Free Trade Agreement was perceived to be bad for Ontario it must, therefore, be good for Quebec.

Therefore, the central question is: can Quebec and Canadian nationalisms be made compatible or are they like two scorpions in a bottle, to use Pierre Vallière's metaphor, destined to destroy each other?

The third question relates to the role of the state. Should the state, rightfully characterized by some as a 'gorging Leviathan', be tamed and submitted to a strict diet? Is the best state the minimum state? Should the glutton become anorexic - or is that in itself a condition as dangerous as obesity? In particular, given free trade and the reduction of federal power, should provincial governments take up the slack or should the free market? Is the latter really 'free' or is it itself dominated by bigness, multinationals and giant conglomerates, absorbing by mergers and acquisitions their smaller brethren?

The fourth question raises the issue of the future of labour and full employment in an increasingly labour-saving technological society. Can informatics create enough jobs to compensate for those which it makes redundant by its amazing efficiency? How far is Canada ready to accept the dislocation of the *new economy* that is emerging in the nineties, full of both threats and intriguing opportunities?

The final question relates to Canada's raison d'être and squarely asks: does Canada have a mission statement that is credible, clear, and the fruit of a national consensus? Or is the country stumbling-along, muddling-through regardless, until the future catches up with it? Canada's original mission statement included within it a clear, explicit rejection of the United States. As various authors have put it, Canada aspired to be "not-America" or "other-than-America". This was its historical raison d'être. With free trade and increasing continentalization can that mission statement be maintained or will a new one have to be forged in the nineties?

Part One

WHY CANADA?

"Between Three Oceans:
The Challenge of a Continental Destiny"

(Peter Waite in, Craig Brown, *The Illustrated History of Canada*,
Toronto: Lester and Orpen Dennys, 1987.)

The question "Why Canada?" is of a different sort
from "Why Britain?", " Why France?" or "Why Greece?"
In each of the latter cases, a strong historical tradition
reaching back into long centuries, if not millennia, answers
the question automatically. "Why France?" .` ` ..well,
because it is there. It has a particular culture, a common
language, a strong national sense of identity and a great
deal of history to remember and to celebrate. Those who
would even raise the question "Why France?" would have
to demonstrate why they are doing so and show that there
are new forces at work challenging France's existence.
Perhaps such forces are, indeed, at work in the case of the
European countries about to embark upon a much closer
union after 1992. However, the onus of proof remains
strongly on the questioner.

In Canada's case, the matter is far less
straightforward. There are many indications that the basic
structure of the country has always been fragile. With no
single common language and no single common culture,
Canada's sense of identity is a perennial source of concern.
A relatively young country, with few major historical
events to remember, it is also conditioned by the fact that it
has only one neighbour: the current reigning world

superpower with ten times its population and wealth and a much stronger sense of purpose.

In many senses Canada has been a historical *tour de force* because it has had to cope with a coalescence of forces leading to greater continental integration with the United States. These forces come from geography, demography, technology, economics and culture. They have been kept in check, in the past, by means of two policies: a) opposing a European link to the geopolitical influence of the United States, and b) creating and maintaining a strong centre to keep the country together. In spite of these two counterweights, the external and the internal, Canada's history in the last century and a half can be characterized by two words: "creeping continentalism".

The gradual increase in patterns of integration between the two economies is easily documented. This integration has been kept in check and occasionally delayed by an assortment of Canadian strategies falling under the two main headings of external and internal counterweights. As the European link became weaker, over time, Canada alternated between the temptation to strike a better deal with the United States and/or to create strong "national policies" or "industrial strategies" as they later became known. External diversification measures designed to avoid putting all the 'eggs' in the American basket have been combined with central government nation-building. This combination has allowed the country to maintain an unstable equilibrium which could be likened to a 'hesitation waltz' with the United States.

There are now signs that the 'hesitation waltz' cannot continue indefinitely. We are moving from creeping to galloping continentalism for a number of reasons. First, the Free Trade Agreement, which came into

effect in January 1989, may lead us into higher forms of
economic integration with political spillovers. Second, the
European integration process, likely to cross new
thresholds after 1992, may make that continent look
inward and act even less as a counterweight to the United
States, as far as Canada is concerned. Third, the
resurgence of Quebec nationalism and Western separatism
may increase the centrifugal forces within Canada to much
higher levels. These factors, coupled with a decentralizing
trend in the Constitution, may further weaken the centre.
Fourth, the arrival of many new immigrants will underline
Canada's identity problem and force the country to define,
or redefine, itself in a meaningful fashion.

All this leads-up to the increasing relevance of
the question "Why Canada?"   In this first part of the book
we analyze, in detail, how this question finds its roots in
Canadian history and geography and why it is likely to
dominate the nineties.

Chapter 1

FREE TRADE IN LONG-TERM PERSPECTIVE

A Questionable Question

If the North American continent were inhabited by 275 million "Vespuccians" and these Vespuccians were perfectly mobile and ethnically homogeneous, there would never have been a free trade debate. It was Amerigo Vespucci, as it will be remembered, who gave his name to the New World and not Christopher Columbus, who actually discovered Cuba. Since the United States has, for all intents and purposes, appropriated the first name of Vespucci and given it very specific national connotations, "American" cannot really be used to describe the entire continent. The Canadian penchant for the adjective "North American" to describe an entity that includes both the United States and Canada, remains unconvincing to the outside observer. After all, in a strict geographical sense, North America must also include Mexico. Yet this is rarely the case when one talks, for instance, about the "North American" lifestyle or economic system. In addition, "North American" often means to the outside observer just "second-class United States" or, "imitation United States", in the same way that the "Latins" of ancient Italy were considered second-class Romans.

A neutral North America could conceivably have been referred to as "Vespuccia" in the same way that "Europe" describes not an enlarged France or Germany but a vast and diversified continent. If "Vespuccia" had, in fact, existed even a rudimentary understanding of economics would have revealed that Vespuccian free trade would be best for all. No one would dream of setting up an artificial and illogical frontier at the 49th parallel and configuring a continental political system featuring sixty-two governments (two federal, fifty state and ten provincial) and at least three major linguistic groups. Drawing a line at the Rio Grande separating Spanish-speaking Mexico from the United States might make some linguistic sense. But the line at the 49th parallel would make no sense, if only economic considerations were to count.

But Vespuccia does not exist, nor is it likely that it ever will. The North American continent was actually colonized by Spaniards, French, and Britons, who then went on to create the economic and political reality which exists today. This reality pre-supposes that we do not assign a zero-value to the political fact of Canada, or to the linguistic fact of French Quebec. If one accepts these constraints, the free trade question becomes infinitely more complex than in the simplistic Vespuccian hypothesis, which was so often assumed by the debaters in the 1988 Canadian federal election.

The complexity of the external challenges facing Canada in this non-Vespuccian continent gives rise to two major issues that must be mentioned in connection with the free trade question. The first one is: to what extent is the Free Trade Agreement with the United States, that was signed in 1989, the proper answer to Canada's structural problems? Should it be the leading light of Canada's future?

The second and perhaps less obvious one is: to what extent is "free trade" itself *a good question?* Asking good questions is a central feature of strategic thinking, since major errors are made when one concentrates on pseudo questions.

In a technical sense, a "pseudo-question" may be defined as one which appears in the wrong place and, in effect, begs itself. In other words, there are sometimes so many implicit assumptions underlying a question, that once the assumptions are accepted, the answer to the question is automatic. If, on the other hand, the assumptions are rejected, the answer cannot be given, one way or the other.

For example, the question "which movie shall we go to" implies an affirmative answer to the previous question "shall we go to the movies tonight?" A negative answer to the first question makes the second irrelevant. Similarly the question, "Shall we see Rocky XIV" may become a pseudo-question if either the film does not exist (in which case the 'no' is automatic) or on the contrary, if it is actually the only movie in town, in which case the 'yes' is automatic. The task of uncovering underlying assumptions behind questions is essential to gaining proper insights on an issue.

The 1988 Free Trade Debate has been dominated by simplistic assumptions at the extremes on both sides. For one extreme, political, cultural and social considerations were given zero value and considered "irrational". Only economic issues counted for that group. For the other extreme, political, social and cultural considerations were given infinite value and economic considerations almost none. Without reliving the election debate of 1988, we can summarize the list of problems that were brought to the fore by the Free Trade Agreement and that remain to be resolved in long-term perspective.

The first concerns the complexity of the Agreement and its lack of transparency for all but the most seasoned experts in international law, economics and diplomacy. As one irate businessman put it: "I was expecting a three-page document. When you have to resort to 1,000 pages to proclaim free trade, obviously there is something wrong."

There is more here than meets the eye. When you couch a document in myriads of legal "whereas" and "notwithstanding" clauses, you are just making sure that a great many lawyers will become rich interpreting the agreement and taking fellow-lawyers to court to discuss their interpretations. In fact, the Agreement's complexity and length are clear signs that a substantial number of potential problems remain submerged. Many of the terms used remain without definition, the most famous of which is the term "subsidy." At least three candidate definitions exist. The Canadian one implicitly-claims that almost no government intervention is a subsidy, as long as it is justified by cultural or regional equalization objectives. The American definition claims that almost any government intervention is a subsidy, except military expenditures and R&D. The "GATT" or General Agreement on Tariffs and Trade holds an intermediate position. Sometime in the nineties, the term will have to be defined.

Beyond the problem of complexity, the Free Trade Agreement has to meet a second and a third line of attack.

The second line of attack *questions the wisdom of basing an export strategy primarily on the signature of a treaty.* It points to the limited value of treaties, and underlines the large number of instruments and policies that governments have to work around them, or to cancel their effects, even after they have been signed.

The third line of attack argues that the 1989 Agreement is the prelude to a much closer economic integration between Canada and the United States, with ultimate political implications. In the natural continuum that goes from "free trade" to an "economic union", there is no real reason for stopping at the free trade stage. The European Economic Community has gone much further and is scheduled to continue along the path to closer economic integration, ultimately reaching full union by 1992.

Let us examine each argument in turn.

Is Signing a Treaty a Good Export Strategy?

Assume for the purposes of argument that the goal of integrating our economy with that of the United States was chosen by national consensus as the top Canadian priority and that it was decided that all energies should be directed towards that objective. A peculiar aspect of the free trade question is that it is quite possible to be in favour of North American economic integration and yet remain against the 1989 Free Trade Agreement. Fundamentally, one must ask the following question: is signing a treaty between two governments a meaningful export strategy, or are there more effective alternatives?

First, consider the background. There has always been a penchant in Canada for blaming our economic ills on outside forces. Canada is not the only country in the world to do so, since the United States has approximately the same penchant. However, interestingly enough, the U.S. and Canadian reactions are diametrical opposite. When faced with economic adversity, the Americans tend to turn inward and become protectionist, while Canada looks outward and seeks freer trade. But whether it is a question of signing a treaty to "obtain secure access to a market" (which is Canada's aspirin when faced with economic uncertainty) or of becoming protectionist (which is the U.S.'s) - in both cases a foreign scapegoat is blamed. Rarely is it acknowledged that the fault might be internal and not external.

The reflex of looking for legal remedies to what are essentially economic ills may itself be an indicator of weakness not strength. It is in marked contrast with, say, the Japanese approach.

For the Japanese, access to world markets is not a question of treaties but one of *competitiveness*. Japan does not formally belong to any significant trade bloc, yet manages to sweep the world with its products, vaulting protectionist barriers as if they were lilliputian hedges. Its quest for competitiveness is so successful that only absolute import quotas and total prohibition of trade can stop it. Japan does not habitually rely on 1,000-page legal agreements to guarantee its access to client markets. A strong economy needs no treaty to export. It exports because its products are considered very competitive and desirable.

In fact, a political honeymoon between two countries is neither a necessary nor a sufficient condition for strong trade links. As evidence, consider for instance the period from 1980 to 1984. This was Trudeau's last term of office and a strongly nationalist Canadian government frequently angered Washington with its policies. Did the U.S. punish Canada by importing less from us? On the contrary, Canadian exports to the United States during this period almost doubled. It was the fastest rate of increase in two decades. In 1984, Canada enjoyed an unprecedented $2 billion surplus with the United States. Political differences did not interfere with the pocket book.

As long as Canadian goods offered good value they were bought by Americans.

Consider now another case when a political honeymoon did exist. When the Parti Québécois was in power in the late seventies, it developed special links with France. The Quebec/France honeymoon was reflected in treaties, fuelled by high-level diplomatic exchanges and was the frequent occasion for cocktail parties, receptions, international conferences and even festivals. However, this honeymoon did not, to the dismay of both parties, amount to a significant increase in transatlantic trade, for the simple reason that businessmen on both sides of the ocean did not see fit to come on board. As we will argue later, this was probably a mistake on both sides, but the fact remains: a political honeymoon is neither a necessary nor a sufficient condition for strong economic links, any more than close friendship is a condition for a successful business transaction.

Second, in considering how meaningful the Free Trade Agreement is, one should note that trade in goods between the United States and Canada was, for all intents and purposes, already 80 percent free in 1986, courtesy of the multilateral GATT Accords and is likely to be 90 percent free in the next round.

In addition, the bilateral trade figures indicate a level of integration of the North American economy that has few parallels elsewhere. By the end of 1985, the volume of trade between the two countries was over $120 billion. Seventy-five percent of Canada's exports went to the United States, while 20 percent of U.S. exports went to Canada. One may be surprised to discover that the United States exported more to Ontario than to Japan and more to British Columbia than to China in that year. In addition, the United States and Canada ranked as the numbers one and two host-nations respectively, in terms of foreign direct investment. The United States was the dominant investor in Canada, while Canada was the fourth largest investor in the United States. In December 1988, before the signature of the Free Trade Agreement, there were of course still some tariffs. Canadian tariffs averaged 9 percent on a third of U.S. exports. U.S. tariffs were even lower and covered a quarter of Canadian exports. Therefore, the popular idea that before free trade, a massive 'Berlin Wall' separated the U.S. and Canadian economies is simply untrue. *There never was such a wall!*

Third, it is also worth noting that the treaty does not really 'secure' access to anything, since future legislation may countermand it. As we noted above, looking for 'secure access' is an admission of weakness. Does your grocer, your mechanic or your tailor try to obtain legally 'secure access' to your business or does he just attempt to attract your business through competitive advantage? Since when is anything 'secure', let alone a foreign market? Besides, in the current North American tête-à-tête, the U.S./Canada marriage is subject to a no-fault divorce clause, which can be obtained at six months' notice, notwithstanding the one thousand legal pages of treaty.

In fact, the only reasonable way of obtaining 'secured access' to a market is to move your business to that market itself.   This is what a number of Canadian companies have done, including such stars as Northern Telecom. If generalized, such movement may signal the flight of capital away from Canada and into the lucrative U.S. market.

The fourth and most telling argument against the concept of basing an export strategy on a treaty is that there are other more influential factors likely to affect our capacity to export to the United States than a signed treaty. These include industrial policies, relative inflation rates, technological advantage and, most important, *exchange rates*. The latter deserve special emphasis.

Assume for a moment two extreme cases. In one, we have complete free trade guaranteed by treaty, but market forces push the Canadian dollar up to par with the American. The United States, tired of facing what it considers an undervalued Canadian dollar, pressures Canada not to interfere with its natural rise. The fact that Canada has enjoyed a strong export surplus with the United States in the 1980-88 period is evidence, in the minds of some Americans, that the Canadian dollar was undervalued. At par, would we still export as much to the United States? It is by no means certain. In the second case, assume free trade breaks down but that the Canadian dollar remains substantially lower than the American, largely because of Canadian central bank policies. Would we necessarily export less to the United States because no treaty had been signed? This is highly unlikely.

The point of this discussion is that *long-term movements in the U.S./Canada exchange rate are likely to be a much stronger factor in determining the nature of trade flows between the two countries than the signature of a treaty.* Interestingly, between October 1987 and February 1989, the Canadian dollar appreciated strongly against its U.S. counterpart, going from 75 cents to almost 84 cents. That 12 percent increase gave Canadian exporters a competitive *disadvantage* with respect to the U.S. market, greater than the projected *advantage* we hope to obtain when all tariffs are abolished between the two countries at the end of the century. Clearly then, the elimination of tariffs plays a very small part among the import-export relationships between the two countries, while exchange rates are a much more significant factor. The only exception to this proposition would be in the case of absolute import quotas being imposed by a protectionist United States. These would limit our export capacity by legally limiting the volume of goods we could send across the border *at any price*. However, this would be tantamount to open trade war and its repercussions would be very serious throughout the world.

It is reasonable to conclude from the foregoing discussion that even if exporting more to the United States were the ultimate objective, the best way to achieve this would be by increasing our competitive advantage - not by signing a fragile treaty which reduces Canada's margin for manoeuvre and which can be cancelled at any time.

This being said, we must not underestimate the *psychological* effects of free trade. Most people still believe in the myth of the past 'Berlin Tariff-Wall' and, therefore, welcome free trade as an expression of new openness in our external relations. Canadian business, for long obsessed with local and regional markets, is being made to discover the lucrative potential south of the border. Similarly, foreign investors, not versed in the intricacies of the GATT Agreement, are genuinely pleased with what they believe is the new Canadian policy and may be more willing to invest in this country with the U.S. market in mind. Quite possibly the psychological arguments in favour of free trade may counterbalance its obvious flaws. However, the massive economic advantages that the Free Trade Agreement is supposed to bring remain highly suspect and more the stuff of electoral rhetoric than sound economics.

Will the Free Trade Agreement Remain Forever 'Just a Commercial Deal'?

An extension of the argument casting doubt on the efficacy of treaties is the further question of whether 'free trade' is the proper final relationship we will have with the United States or whether we will draw even closer. It will be noted that free trade is just the first of five possible stages of integration between nations. These are:

1. A Free Trade Zone. This may be partial or total. Fundamentally it means that there is free movement of goods across international borders. All visible tariff barriers are eliminated but not necessarily non-tariff barriers.

2. A Common Market. Here a free trade zone is augmented by free movements not only of goods but also of *services, capital and technology.* Usually a common market means free movement of people too. If one can sell services across the border it should be possible to physically move across the border or to set up a branch plant.

3. A Customs Union. This is a free trade zone or common market with a common tariff adopted by all parties vis-à-vis the rest of the world. A free trade zone says nothing about common external tariffs against third parties. Thus, under free trade, it would be possible for country "A" to sneak goods into country "B" from a third country, even though the latter is outside the free trade zone. If the United States were to tighten its omnibus protectionist legislation and exempt Canada from it, either this would be an invitation for third countries to sneak goods into the United States through Canada, or it would mean that Canada would have to adopt a common external tariff with the United States. In other words, Canada would have to

become as protectionist with respect to the rest of the world as it was towards the United States.

4. _An Economic Policy Union_. This is a common market with, in addition, a _harmonization of economic policies_ by the member governments. In other words, non-tariff trade barriers emanating from local or national government policies are removed to eliminate artificial distortions to the free movements of people and goods. Taxation policies are also harmonized. Ultimately, monetary policies are also co-ordinated, either by the adoption of a common currency or by linking currencies so tightly that they are, in fact, identical although carrying different names. In the end, an economic policy union ultimately means that there are no _policy-induced_ advantages in locating in a particular place within the union. All locational advantages are natural or cultural in origin. Industries may choose the Sunbelt for the sunshine, or the Boston area for its universities, or the Montreal area for its cosmopolitanism, but none of the choices would be influenced by special tax breaks or subsidies.

5. _A Political Union_. The final stage in international integration is a political union which may take the form of a loose confederation, a tighter federation or, more rarely, a new unitary state.

 Will integration with the United States stop at free trade? Free trade is a sort of Parti Québécois-style "sovereignty-association" with our southern neighbour. Can it stay at that level?   There are strong reasons to believe that the answer is 'no'. As the nineties progress, free trade will have to move to higher forms of integration.

Is a North American Common Market likely in the Nineties?

We already have many of the features of a common market between Canada and the United States. It will be remembered that a common market implies the free movement of factors of production across international borders. There are four groups of productive factors: natural resources, capital, technology and people. The first three are already moving between the two countries quite freely. Whatever impediments exist come more from non-tariff barriers than from official economic policies. The only one that is still subject to restrictions is the free movement of people. This is where the question of free trade in services comes into play.

If services are not allowed to move freely across the border, then the Free Trade Agreement will ultimately mean very little, because of the fact that both the United States and Canada are now primarily service economies. The so-called "tertiary" or service sector accounts for well over half the total output in each country. Clearly, unless services are fully included, the Free Trade Agreement will not change much. The Agreement itself is ambiguous on this subject but, as times progress, most services are likely to be allowed to move freely across the border. When this is achieved, the next step will be temporary, and then more permanent, population movements.

Once population movements are allowed across the international border, (something which will be fully achieved in Europe in 1992) interesting questions will arise. First, this will probably force Canada and the United States to harmonize their immigration policies. If not, would-be immigrants to the United States will come in through Canada - as many would have done in the past had it not been for stricter U.S. laws. Second, there will be some population exchange. A number of Canadians, immigrant or native-born, will seek the more temperate climates of the Sunbelt, and a number of Americans may move north to Canada in search of a 'new frontier'. The net migration balance is probably going to be negative for Canada and the country is likely to suffer a population loss. However, if it does not, then the American component of Canada's population will increase, thus making it more probable that closer political ties between the two countries will be envisioned.

The ultimate possibility of people moving freely across the 49th parallel is the single most important aspect of the free trade question. At present, this movement is forbidden. If, however, the economic integration process succeeds, it is difficult to imagine how free trade in services, and the migratory movements consequent to such trade, can be perpetually disallowed. Yet, once free migration is accepted, the long-term political viability of Canada will become much more questionable.

Is an Economic Policy Union
Likely in the Nineties ?

With a common market, especially a successful one, the question of policy harmonization becomes increasingly pressing. A common market which gives free reign to independent policies by the governments within it could lead to utter confusion. There are, as noted earlier, sixty-two governments in the U.S./Canada zone - two federal, ten provincial and fifty state. The power of U.S. states is limited by both the U.S. constitution, which is much more centralist than Canada's, and by a non-interventionist tradition. Even so, distortions introduced by state non-tariff barriers in the United States and provincial non-tariff barriers in Canada are currently strong. Since Canada is a confederal rather than a federal union, the provinces have considerably more powers than their United States counterparts. In addition, in the spirit of the Meech Lake Accord, the 'distinct' nature of each of Canada's two founding nations could become the legitimate basis for great divergences in provincial public policies. If one were to add to the provincial governments the municipal ones, further public sector-induced distortions to 'free' trade could be envisioned. Interestingly, the United States specified, in 1987, that it wished the active support not only of the provincial but also of the municipal Canadian governments, thus recognizing and fearing that possibility.

Some sort of external tariff harmonization will also have to be considered. If the United States strengthens its protectionist legislation, it will probably request a customs union with Canada. A 'free economic zone', subject to the diverging public policies of multiple governments, will *in the end* be neither 'free' nor an 'economic zone'. To avoid such confusion, the pressure for harmonization will be very strong indeed.

When harmonization finally occurs, it will naturally follow the U.S. pattern. It is implausible that, in an integrated North American economy of the non-"Vespuccian" variety, the United States will bend its laws and regulations to fit a Canadian agenda. It is much more likely that the junior partner, Canada, whose entire population matches only that of California, will have to accept the senior partner's priorities.

Other economic policies will likely follow the same pattern as monetary policies have, where the Canadian dollar follows the U.S. dollar up or down in world markets, and Canadian interest rates have always remained close to the American ones. Taxation policies will also have to be harmonized. Otherwise, with the free movement of services and people in a common market, everyone will flock to the lower taxation areas. Unless constrained by very strong nationalist feelings, many Canadians and Québécois will trade their higher marginal tax rates for more appealing lower U.S. rates.

If the harmonization of economic policies is a logical and desirable sequel to the institution of a common market, what about political integration? When would that make sense? Proponents of free trade with the United States assure us that this can never be placed on the table. They point to the European Economic Community and argue that there was no cession of sovereignty there. Upon analysis, these arguments can be shown to be very superficial, for two reasons.

First, the Treaty of Rome, which created the European Economic Community in 1958, clearly specified that ultimate political union was the goal. The Europeans rejected the free trade alternative to their common market. True enough, the rival European Free Trade Zone has co-existed with the EEC. Britain was a member of the former but not of the latter for many years. But in the seventies, it was clear that the 'community' idea was triumphing over the 'free trade zone' idea. Britain, together with other dissident countries, joined the EEC.

Since its inception in 1958, the European Economic Community has made great strides towards political as well as economic policy harmonization, and this has manifested itself in some concrete achievements. The political integration process remains very slow. It may take the rest of this century, or more, to become complete but it is certainly on the agenda. The watershed year is supposed to be 1992, after which all non-tariff barriers will have to be permanently eliminated from European public policies, as far as intra-European trade is concerned. If political integration has not yet been achieved, it is because of strong surviving national antagonisms, but no one has officially advocated that it should not be achieved. It would be the crowning finale to the European integration process, *officially* wished by all but slow to implement.

The only previous European example of political integration following economic took over forty years to realize. The German states formed a *Zollverein* or customs union in 1830, and only achieved political union in 1871, at the conclusion of the Franco-Prussian War. It took forty years for a nation speaking only one language to unite into one state. It will probably take at least as long for Europe, beset with a history of internal wars. But since the objective of the EEC is political integration, whether successful or not, it cannot be a model for North American free trade, where political integration is not on the official agenda.

The second point which invalidates the comparison between Canada and the United States on the one hand, and the EEC on the other, is the question of relative size. Within the EEC, there are four large countries which balance each other out: Germany, France, Britain and Italy. The smaller countries of Europe have maintained their historical independence through that balance of power. In the eighteenth and nineteenth centuries, many wars were fought over the smaller countries, and the principle of balance of power was enshrined in the European political system. This system has now been effectively transposed as a modus operandi within the European Community.

In contrast, the Canada/United States relationship, as will be shown in the following chapter, is geopolitically very different. The size differential is enormous and there are no North American counterweights. A comparable European situation would pit Poland against Russia, Holland against West Germany, or Monaco against France. In these unequal relationships, where one country is so obviously the senior partner, the preservation of the smaller country's full sovereignty is very difficult. Monaco's independence from France is largely symbolic and Poland's from Russia (until very recently) painfully non-existent. Holland, for sure, would rather fight than have a one-on-one integration with West Germany.

The 'spillover' thesis, that free trade will spillover into a common market and a common market into an economic and ultimately a political union, has a further argument in its favour: Canada's long-term interests once the economic integration process becomes irreversible. In the long run, once the two countries are so intertwined as to have virtually indistinguishable economies, *it will be in Canada's interest to seek political union* - and probably in the United States' interest to drag its feet on that request. The reason is simple.

If the key economic and political decisions are taken south of the border, surely it would make sense to send twenty Canadian senators to Washington rather than none at all. Obviously, it is not sure that the United States would welcome twenty new senators from north of the border, but from Canada's point of view it would be a plus. Therefore, somewhere along the line, and especially if economic integration is successful, political union will have to be envisioned, and Canada is likely to be the petitioner on that one.

The United States will studiously avoid an annexationist image and will receive Canada's application to join without enthusiasm. However, on the U.S. side too, the prospect of a politically unified North America may become very appealing, and an enlarged United States is not an unthinkable finale to the process which is presently unfolding. In fact, this finale, perhaps a generation away, is rooted in the history of this continent, as the next chapter will demonstrate.

Chapter 2

THE CHALLENGE OF A
CONTINENTAL DESTINY

Beneath the tip of the iceberg of free trade is the real question that has dominated Canadian history from its inception: how to develop a meaningful relationship with the United States without being absorbed by them. The accomplishment of this feat has been an enormous challenge for Canada. It has two principal dimensions - one geopolitical and one historical.

"Geopolitics" is a science which describes how power politics is conditioned by geography: it shows how geographical factors can affect political relations among nations, regions, or social entities existing in physical space. Its importance was first recognized by the British geographer Macinder and further developed by the German historian Karl Haushofer (1896-1946). It was and is very influential in explaining global power relationships and how national foreign policies are formed. One of its applications in the North American context is to examine the viability of political configurations in terms of centre-periphery relations, location theory and gravitational forces.

Canada's geopolitical challenge is, simply stated, its continuing attempt to resist the gravitational pull of the neighbour to the immediate south. In the last two centuries, Canada has managed that feat by two methods taken singly or in combination: the first was externally based and consisted of *opposing a European counterweight to the U.S. colossus.* This counterweight was provided by France in the sixteenth and seventeenth centuries against what was then the Thirteen Colonies, and then by Britain against the United States in the nineteenth and twentieth centuries. Whenever that counterweight faltered, either because the European power had just lost a war, or because it was increasingly unwilling to play the role of counterweight, the region that is now Canada felt irresistibly drawn to the region that is now the United States. At those difficult moments, variants of the second method were envisioned: an *internal counterweight* based on the idea of a strong national economy backed by a powerful central government. In the remaining pages of this chapter we will examine the magnitude of the geopolitical challenge and briefly retrace how Canada has managed, so far, to juggle its way out of joining the United States by the use of both counterweights, the external and the internal.

The Geographical Imperative

At the root of the Canadian dilemma is the overwhelming importance of geography. In John A. Macdonald's famous saying, Canada was described as having "too much geography and too little history." More apt a statement to characterize Canada is difficult to find. Historian Arthur Lower enlarged: "From the land must come the soul of Canada". Northrop Frye remarked, "Central to Canadian writing is the imminence of the natural world." Margaret Atwood declared, "Much of Canadian character comes from 'northerness' blended with Mediterranean immigration and a quasi-Mediterranean charter culture, the French Canadian." (Quotations from Richard Gwyn, *The 49th Paradox,* p. 182). Pierre Dansereau, the eminent Canadian ecologist once stated with compelling simplicity, "The dominant trend in Canada is... winter." A contemporary political scientist attempted to describe Canada's international stance as a middle power and came up with the paradox that Canada was "a regional power ... without a region." Yet politicians and analysts have been strangely silent on this most important feature of the Canadian reality in the Free Trade Debate.

Why is geography so important? Its overwhelming influence in Canadian life can be attributed to the interplay of six factors: size, climate, a small population, uneven population density, a natural Atlantic rather than Pacific orientation, and proximity to the United States. Taken singly, any of these factors, which exist in other countries, could be discounted and neutralized. Taken jointly, the six factors add-up to, or more precisely 'multiply-up to' a geopolitical challenge with few equals throughout the world - one which, in some form or other, permeates all aspects of Canadian life.

Size

As Clive Simmonds, the noted Canadian futurist, once said, "We are not a country. We are a continent trying to be a country. If everything in Canada were halved, everything would go better." In a more direct sense, many analyses of Canadian issues hover around a paradoxical duality: Canada is both too large and too small.

As the second largest country in the world after Russia, Canada has enormous size. In purchasing power it is the ninth largest country in the world, right after Italy. It absorbs over 20 percent of U.S exports. But its total population is comparable to that of the state of California.

This severely constrains the possibility of economies of scale from internal markets and makes import-substitution policies quite unrealistic. Unlike Brazil, with 100 million internal consumers to tap, Canada can only muster 25 million, spread all over the land and with diverse interests and traditions.

The enormous size of the land immediately places the focus on *transport* and *communication,* the true backbones of Canada. It is not surprising that this country developed world-class expertise in these twin fields. The transportation infrastructure was correctly seen, in the late nineteenth century, as a 'make' or 'break' challenge for Canada. The primary motivating force behind the construction of the national railways was the realization that without the Canadian transcontinentals, economic links between Eastern and Central Canada on the one hand, and the West on the other, would go through U.S. railways. This would ultimately deal a death-blow to Canada's viability as a nation.

Similarly, the communication infrastructure was seen as a nation-building instrument. It is no coincidence that Canada has been in the forefront of technological innovations in this field, ranging from telephony to cable distribution, fiber optics and satellite transmission. If there is now a 'world electronic highway', as some people argue, the Canadian input to the construction of that highway has been significant. In this important area the country has certainly made its mark.

But, sadly, neither the transportation nor the communication infrastructures have helped to meet fully the challenge of size. Many of Canada's smaller cities and towns are on the periphery - marginalized from the mainstream and isolated from the large urban areas. Flying over these remote areas often gives an eerie feeling of strangeness: miles of wilderness suddenly broken by a few parking lots, some buildings here and there and then ... more miles of wilderness. The transcontinental railways have never been bursting with activity and have been in structural decline for some time now. The Trans-Canada Highway is largely empty over long stretches. Cable distribution, in some senses a Canadian first, has succeeded in bringing many television channels into Canadian homes but what do these channels carry? Principally U.S. programmes

The size of the country has also had its effect on ideas. As Robert Fulford stated in *Canada, A Landscape Portrait 1982*, "When they arrive in Canada, political ideas change ... They are dissipated by the size of the land. For this reason Canada offers an especially frustrating life to intellectuals whose training is based on European or American models. They almost always break their sword." (cited in Gwyn, *The 49th Paradox*).

Climate

Canada's climate is another important element in the puzzle. Most of the country is subjected to intense variations in temperature. Montreal is colder than Leningrad in the winter and on some summer days as hot as Cairo. The winter snowstorms are sometimes matched by summer rains in their severity, as for instance the torrential downpour of July 14, 1987 in Montreal. The climate brings with it disruptions: airline, rail and road delays, clogged city streets, power failures and in general, considerable expenditures to meet its challenges. A sizeable portion of Canadian incomes must be spent fighting the climate - expenses range from heating bills, to large amounts spent on wardrobes, to frequent changes in cars that succumb prematurely to rust or mechanically break-down long before they would in California or Florida.

The long and heavy Canadian winter has, historically, deterred all but the adventurous from settling here. It is also a leading cause of north to south emigration, whether of the temporary variety (the annual pilgrimage to Florida) or the more permanent one (French-Canadian emigration to New England). Voltaire called Canada "quelques arpents de neige." Today, in spite of high technology, that is exactly what Canada remains to many foreign observers.

The climate, more than anything else, has slowed immigration and kept the population from ever reaching an economically-viable size. If Canada had a Mediterranean or Western European climate, it is reasonable to suppose that the land would have filled-up like the United States and that in 1988 there would have been 200 million Canadians, allowing the country to claim superpower status.

Population

The small numbers of Canadians today represent only one part of the population problem. We are only 25 million in the second largest country in the world but, in addition, those 25 million are poorly distributed across the land. Ninety percent of them live in a thin belt within 200 kilometres of the Unites States border. This, more than any other demographic fact, lends credence to Canada's image as being within the periphery of the United States and not having a separate existence. The bulk of the country, its middle and northern parts, is very sparsely inhabited.

Valiant attempts to design and develop a 'mid-Canada corridor,' have never come to fruition.

The uneven north-south distribution of Canada's population is exacerbated by two other unbalanced ratios: east-west and urban-rural. The east-west ratios are, of course, strongly favourable to the east. Ontario and Quebec represent more than half the Canadian population. This gives disproportionate political power to these two provinces and inevitably leads to the under-representation of the Atlantic and Western provinces in Ottawa. This fact was in the process of being altered in the seventies, when oil-rich Alberta attracted population away from Ontario and Quebec. But with the end of the oil boom, central Canada has regained its economic, political and cultural dominance, and retained its population base.

Demographic density imbalance creates one of the major internal problems of Canada – *regional disparities,* – and places the central government before a dilemma. *If it accepts the natural logic of the market which tends to empty the peripheral, non-resource rich provinces in favour of the central industrial ones, regional disparities will further increase. If the central government opposes these market forces it must introduce artificial distortions which, in a national sense, create waste.* The historical behaviour of Canadian central governments has been to choose the latter policy and attempt to reduce regional disparities. The trend of the future is unclear. Although central governments will continue to pay lip service to regional equalization, the combined effect of the Free Trade Agreement and the Meech Lake Accord could slowly alter these policies.

The other feature of population distribution that is problematic is the urban-rural split. Canadians are, by and large, much more urbanized than Americans. The typical Canadian lives in a larger city than his American counterpart. In fact, almost half of all Canadians live in the urban corridor which stretches from Québec City to Windsor, Ontario around an axis that is demographically anchored by Toronto and Montreal. This is the hub of central Canada where all decisions are really made and where elections are won or lost. Appropriately, Ottawa-Hull, the National Capital, is close to the centre of this axis and straddles Ontario and Quebec. Beyond the Quebec-Windsor corridor the rest of Canada is made-up of small pockets of civilization in a vast expanse of natural wilderness.

Atlantic rather than Pacific Orientation

Another geographical aspect which has conditioned the evolution of Canada is the North American continent's Atlantic rather than Pacific orientation. If the continent had a face and eyes these would naturally be pointing east towards the Atlantic, rather than west towards the Pacific. Canada and the United States were settled by European immigrants so the geographical 'doors and windows' face the Atlantic. From the sixteenth to the nineteenth century, settlers followed the waterways. Transportation by water is easier than over land and in penetrating a continent there is a tendency to follow the waterways. There are four major waterways linking the heart of North America with the East Coast and none of importance on the West Coast. The first settlement path was the St. Lawrence Valley, which allowed the immigrant waves from Europe to go as far as the Great Lakes. The economic development of Canada, which was closely tied to the fur trade and the pursuit of the beaver, allowed the traders to move further inland. In this context, Montreal enjoyed the status of being the premier entry point into North America, since it is a thousand miles inland from the Atlantic Ocean.

The fur trade, providing one of the first Canadian staple exports, also used another route: the northern one through Hudson Bay, made famous by the Hudson's Bay Company. However, as the continent developed, the southern routes became dominant. These included the Hudson River route in New England, which eventually linked up with the Great Lakes through the Erie Canal, and the Mississippi, which opened up Louisiana. The region to the east of the arc defined by Hudson Bay and the St. Lawrence to the north, the Mississippi to the south and centred on the Great Lakes, constituted the heartland of North America until about 1850, when the West started to open up.

North America's Atlantic, rather than Pacific, orientation was further strengthened by the fact that the Pacific is twice the size of the Atlantic. The 'pond' was for two centuries the centre of the world economy. *Present trends point increasingly to the Pacific but, for good or for ill, Canadian geography is much more turned towards Europe and the Atlantic than towards Japan and the Pacific.* It should be observed that even with today's jet travel, St. John's, Newfoundland is about three hours away from Prestwick, Scotland while Japan is more than four times as far from Vancouver. This Atlantic orientation of the North American continent has been the principal reason for its colonization by Europeans rather than by Asians.

Proximity to the United States

Canada's proximity to the United States is, of course, the major feature of its geographical reality.

Assume, for purposes of argument, that instead of the United States there were many small countries south of the border, or a large ocean. Most assuredly, Canada's history would have been very different, even if all other factors had remained constant. But there is no ocean south of the border. There is a huge and very dynamic country.

Elsewhere in the world one can find many small countries co-habiting in close proximity with much larger ones. Elsewhere, one can also find countries that are highly dualistic, if not pluralistic. But the *combination of the two,* internal dualism generating strong centrifugal forces and external gravitational pulls from a neighbour ten-times as large, spells enormous challenge. The geopolitical imbalances created by the conjunction of these two forces could lead to the breaking up of the smaller country.

The Historical Counterweight.

The weight of geography has forced Canada into a fundamental choice that it believes it has already made and yet, in some senses, it has never made. In a two century-long 'hesitation waltz', Canada has 'dilly-dallied' and 'fudged' on whether it should draw closer to the United States and even join it, or alternatively carve out a separate existence for itself north of the 49th parallel. Politicians will tell us that the choice has been made. Canada is separate and wants to remain so. Reality tells us that there is perennial ambivalence.

Because of the structural imbalance between the Canadian and U.S economies, a precondition for the existence of Canada as a truly separate nation is the presence of a meaningful counterweight to the United States. Historically, the counterweight has been European in origin. First the French, then the British, have provided Canada with economic, political and cultural countervails to U.S influence. But the pendulum has experienced wide swings and has manifested itself by periodic rapprochements with the United States, followed by periods of anti-Americanism.

Overall, Canada has alternated between three major geopolitical stances:
• The Quest for A Separate Existence backed by an (external) European Counterweight;
• The Quest for A Separate Existence based on an (internal) Nationalist Counterweight;
• The American Option - partial or full integration with the United States.

In the search for the 'great compromise', none of these were ever fully chosen and none totally rejected. But in terms of historical development, the Canadian responses to the geopolitical challenge went through four phases.

The first phase covered the era of French mercantilism, from Samuel de Champlain's founding of Québec in 1608 to the defeat of Montcalm on the Plains of Abraham in 1759. The second phase relied strongly on a European counterweight, in the form of a powerful British Empire, which lasted until about 1846, the date of the repeal of the British Corn Laws, and then it declined steadily thereafter. The third phase started with Confederation, in 1867, and attempted a counterweight from within, supported by the strength of the British Empire. When the latter ceased to be either British or an empire, after the Suez débacle in 1956, Canada slowly moved to the fourth phase in which we are still living: the quest for identity and the development of an internal counterweight.

Let us look at this historical script to understand the present debates, because in this matter, as in so many others, "plus ça change et plus c'est la même chose."

Phase I : Banking on French Mercantilism (1600-1763)

Canada, as it will be remembered, was first colonized by French-speaking Europeans, for the most part subjects of the King of France. In the sixteenth, seventeenth and eighteen centuries, the European scramble for North America left Britain and Holland with what is today the Eastern United States, Spain with Florida and France with the St. Lawrence Valley. The principal staple export of the latter was the fur trade. But, as a generation of Canadian economic historians, led by Harold Innis, has shown, the economic linkages of the fur trade were too weak to support a growing population. A few *coureurs de bois*, a few traders and some support services here were all that was needed to maintain the lucrative but non-permanent trade - a trade which, in the minds of European businessmen, was second only to gold in terms of profitability.

Mercantilism was the dominant political and economic theory of the times. It argued that the state should intervene to allow the nation to obtain balance of payments surpluses that would take the form of gold and silver reserves. It also argued that a strong state should possess colonies in order to increase its global economic and political power. In French mercantilist thinking, the most eloquent exponent of which was Jean Baptiste Colbert, the Intendant of Louis XIV, North America was a great prize. Notwithstanding Canada's inclement climate and its small population, the French mercantilists called it 'New France', thereby giving it top-ranking among the colonies. In Colbert's vision, New France could and should expand westward and southwards in order to dominate North America, which, the Intendant believed, could ultimately become French-speaking and an extension of France. To accomplish this aim, the expansion of the English-speaking American colonies westwards had to be stopped. The best way to stop it was to occupy the previously-mentioned arc covering the area from the St. Lawrence Valley in the north to the Mississippi and anchored on the Great Lakes. To be credible, this arc of containment had to be densely populated by either Frenchmen or Francisized native peoples.

At the heart of the first European counterweight was, therefore, a population policy. Colbert and Louis XIV tried everything to settle the land. Incentives, subsidies, tax holidays, Francisization policies for native people were all used to win the demographic battle. It was a precursor of the twentieth-century Québécois *revanche des berceaux*. But it did not succeed. For various reasons, some connected with climate, others with lack of proximity to markets, the attempt to create a diversified, French-speaking and densely-populated super-New France combining Canada and Louisiana failed. By the time the final military reckoning of the Seven Years War came about in 1756, there were fewer than 60,000 French-speaking *Habitants* in Canada to oppose over 2 million English-speaking Americans. The unequal war had to be lost by France. It was mathematical. Even if Montcalm had won the 1759 Battle of the Plains of Abraham, he or his successors would have been defeated elsewhere.

After contributing to the initial economic development of Canada, for almost two centuries, and backing the expansion of the fur trade through state

intervention, France acknowledged defeat and gave-up
Canada in order to keep the French Antilles. Faced with
this first failure of the European counterweight, the
French-speaking *Habitants,* now abandoned by France,
sought the protection of the King of Britain against the
religious intolerance of the Protestant, American Colonies.
Phase I was over. The French counterweight was now
replaced by the British.

Phase II : Betting on Britain (1763-1867)

After the United States had declared its
independence and won the Revolutionary War against
Britain, *anti-Americanism became the raison d'être of
Canada.* Canada was that part of British North America
which refused to join the United States, and those
Americans who wished to remain British migrated north to
Canada. Thus 50,000 United Empire Loyalists came to
Canada in 1784 and became the first major wave of
English Canadian settlement.

Since that time, Canadian politics has revolved
along two axes, English versus French and Canada versus
the United States. As Richard Gwyn puts it: "Throughout
most of its history, Canada's raison d'être was to be 'not-
America'." Or, as the American historian Bartlett Brebner
put it: "The most striking thing about Canada is that it did
not become part of the United States. In the beginning, it
was a very close thing. Britain, having conquered New
France, almost gave it up, in 1759, for sugar-rich
Guadeloupe. Had it done so, there would not have been an
'other' America for the Loyalists to go to." (Gwyn, p. 21)

Nevertheless, in the early post-revolutionary
period, many supporters of the U.S. revolution believed in
an early form of 'manifest destiny'.

Two groups of American revolutionaries invaded the St. Lawrence in 1775 (before the Declaration of Independence in Philadelphia). There was some resistance from Francophone Quebec. France supported the United States but Quebec supported Britain, in order to retain a religious freedom that appeared threatened by the States.

It should be noted that the first Constitution of the United States (the Articles of Confederation) extended a special standing invitation to Canada to join (Article 11). In 1775, the Continental Congress invited Canada to become part of the Union and then sent Benedict Arnold to conquer Quebec. But Arnold had too few troops and the *Canadiens'* loyalty was to the Crown. The Articles of Confederation (1781) of the thirteen colonies had declared Canada "entitled to all the advantages of the Union."

For decades after the revolution, U.S. leaders like John Adams and Henry Clay had the dual ambition of both ousting Britain from North America and expanding the United States northward. The U.S./Canada population ratio at the time was 20/1 versus 10/1 now.

In 1803, Jefferson bought Louisiana from Napoleon for $15 million and United States interests looked to the south. But in 1812, spillovers from the European conflict reached North America and the United States and Canada fought a brief war. With Britain's help, Canada defeated the United States and on August 24, 1814, the British burnt the presidential mansion and some government offices in Washington. The Anglo-American Treaty of 1818, which ended the war, ironed-out problems and established the border along the 49th parallel.

After 1812, the prevailing attitude in the United States was that Canada should be annexed peacefully, when it 'came to its senses' and realized that joining the

United States was its 'ultimate salvation'. Meanwhile, between 1815 and 1845, the United States acquired Florida, Texas and the Oregon and Mexican Territories, adding 1.3 million square miles to the nation. At the same time, the U.S population tripled from 8.5 million in 1815 to 22 million in 1848. In the Mexican War of 1846-1848, the United States took, by conquest, areas which now comprise New Mexico, Arizona, California, Nevada and Utah. In 1867, Russia sold Alaska to the United States for $7.2 million, thereby adding another half a million square miles of real estate, an area twice the size of Texas.

In 1840 the expression 'manifest destiny' was coined by an American journalist, John L Sullivan. He wrote: "The United States has the manifest destiny to overspread the continent allotted by Providence to the free development of our yearly multiplying millions." The Manifest Destiny doctrine was used to justify the U.S. takeover of the northern-half of Mexico. In the mid 1840s, James Gordon Benett said "All we want is Canada to join us." In 1846, an Indiana Congressman declared: "The U.S. is bound to extend from the Isthmus of Darien to the Straits of Bering."

Throughout the period from 1783 to 1846, the European counterweight remained strong. Britain ruled the seas and, through appropriate alliances, Europe as well. In America, it acted as the guarantor of Canadian independence in the north and of South American independence from Spain and Portugal in the south. But Britain's economic success led it to doubt the relevance of an old-style mercantilist empire. Strengthened by its Industrial Revolution, it was the Japan of the times, outcompeting almost everyone. Under these circumstances, imperial protectionism was not essential.

As a gesture of self-confidence and as an expression of faith in international specialization (the true 'wealth of nations' according to Adam Smith), Britain repealed the Corn Laws in 1846. The Corn Laws were British protectionist laws allowing wheat to be imported into Britain only when its price reached a certain level. The Corn Laws favoured British self-sufficiency within the Empire. When however, the British Industrial Revolution allowed that country to focus on secondary manufacturing and more or less abandon agricultural self-sufficiency, it chose to move from a protectionist to a free trade stance. This signalled the beginning of the end of colonial mercantilism. Britain would import its food and export industrial commodities on the open market. It meant a weakening of the imperial connection for Canada.

Feeling once again abandoned by their European partner, a number of Montreal businessmen started lobbying for union with the United States. To prevent the growth of this movement, Lord Elgin approached the Americans to sign a free trade accord. Eight years of on-again off-again negotiations took place, with a good deal of American indifference. The Elgin-Marcy Reciprocity Treaty was ultimately signed in 1854. The Treaty was comprehensive and permitted the free exchange of a large number of products. It instituted free navigation and sectoral free trade in natural products.

The Reciprocity Treaty of 1854 marks the first major swing of the Canadian pendulum to the American side. The weakening of the European link drove Canada right into the arms of the United States. But the accord was destined to be short-lived. Although Canada did its part and moved its economy closer to that of its southern neighbour by changing, among other things, the name of its currency from the pound to the dollar, the American Civil War put a stop to the integration process. Before the Civil War, the Southern states were fearful of admitting more slavery-free states into the Union. During the Civil War, Britain, with typical divide-and-rule international diplomacy, decided to support the South against the North. When the North finally won the war, it retaliated against Britain by abrogating, in 1866, the Reciprocity Treaty. At that time, the United States had the largest army in the world - 800,000 strong, battle seasoned and fresh from the triumph against the Secessionists. It could have marched over Canada unopposed and achieved what it had failed to do in 1812.

Phase III: Counting on Confederation and the British Empire (1867- 1956)

The period 1867 to 1956 marks the full blossoming of the Canadian dilemma: *how to face a United States geopolitical challenge that is being steadily exacerbated by the slow but inexorable weakening of the European counterweight.* To meet this increasingly-large problem, Canada alternated between its three major policy thrusts: cajoling and entreating the United States into Free Trade Agreements; opposing whatever was left of the European counterweight to U.S. annexationist ambitions; and rebuilding from within by trying-out an internal counterweight. Annexationist moves were sporadic and only half-hearted because of a U.S. respect for Canada's Anglo-Saxon heritage and a lingering fear of Britain, still the world's only superpower.

The Confederation of 1867 was the first major attempt at an internal counterweight. Fearful of the Americans and feeling abandoned by Britain, the Canadian provinces decided to try for a strong Canada to avoid absorption by the United States. This led to Confederation, a decision by the provinces to hang together in the face of mounting external threats. But, in order to avoid the possibility of a U.S.-style civil war, the Canadian leaders opted for a looser confederation, with shared sovereignty among the provinces and the federal government, rather than a full federation ceding ultimate power to the central authority as was the case in the United States. Thus, after 1867, two political federations co-existed in North America: a strong American federation, fresh from its victory over its internal separatists, the Southern states; and a weaker Canadian one, dividing sovereignty among the participants and recognizing even then, in its own way, the 'distinct' character of French Canada.

As part of the picture, indeed essential to it, was a new version of the European counterweight - now increasingly more legal and ceremonial than political and economic, but still meaningful nevertheless. Canada did not seek to declare its independence. It would have been foolhardy to do so. It opted to remain part of the British Empire and to seek its moral and legal protection. The Articles of Confederation were enshrined in an Act of the British Parliament, known as the British North America Act. This piece of legislation functioned as Canada's constitution until Pierre Trudeau patriated it in 1981.

'Rebuilding from within' took early form in John A. Macdonald's National Policy which, in contemporary terminology, would be called an 'industrial strategy'. But before the industrial strategy became the centrepiece of Canadian development planning, there was, first, another attempt to mend the fences with the United States and second, a campaign to enlarge Confederation. Revivals of

Reciprocity were tried in 1869, 1871, and 1874 but each of these attempts failed because of U.S. introversion after the Civil War. On the other hand, the expansion of Confederation brought in Nova Scotia in 1868, in spite of its anti-Canadian and separatist provincial legislature, and Prince Edward Island in 1873. John A. Macdonald's National Policy was a reaction to the 1874 free trade failure, ultimately blocked by the United States Senate. It featured two major policy instruments: the building of a strong Canadian transportation infrastructure, in the form of a transcontinental railway, and the establishment of a high external tariff to keep jobs in Canada. One of the major threats to Canada, at the time, was not U.S. annexation, but voluntary assimilation as Canadians emigrated en masse to the United States. Between 1870 and 1914, two million Canadians moved to the United States, many of them French Canadians. The offspring of the United Empire Loyalists and of the *Habitants* decided to vote with their feet and become American.

Between 1887 and 1891, a 'pre-play' of the 1988 Free Trade Debate took place in Canada, this time with the Liberals of Sir Wilfrid Laurier in favour and the Conservatives of John A. Macdonald against. Then, as in 1988, omnibus U.S. protectionist bills loomed on the horizon. In that particular instance, the protectionist forces won on both sides of the border. The United States adopted the highly-protectionist McKinley Act in 1890, and Laurier's liberals were soundly defeated in the 1891 federal election. The National Policy soared into full flight and remained the dominant Canadian federal policy until 1911. In that year, the Liberals of Sir Wilfrid Laurier, back in power, negotiated a new Free Trade Treaty, much more comprehensive than that of 1854 and very advantageous to

Canada. It was ratified by the United States Senate but was ultimately rejected by the Canadian voters in a federal election that brought Robert Borden's Conservatives to power.

From 1911 to 1935, Canada and the United States co-existed, side by side, without any major re-opening of the free trade talks. In 1930, after the Great Crash of 1929, U.S. protectionism surfaced once again and took the form of yet another omnibus anti-import bill, the Smoot-Hawley Tariff, which helped precipitate the Great Depression. Tariffs were raised by 59 percent, and, by 1932, this had reduced imports to the level of 1909. Unemployment in the United States went up to 25 percent and per capita income dropped to 1907 levels.

In 1935, as part of Roosevelt's New Deal, the United States loosened its protectionism and, between 1935 and 1938, signed two reciprocity agreements with Canada. This led to a third in 1941, the Ogdenburg Agreement and a fourth in 1944, instituting free trade in agricultural commodities. In 1947, Truman and Mackenzie-King opened negotiations for comprehensive free trade, but in 1948 Mackenzie-King ended the negotiations. At about that time, international GATT-sponsored negotiations to end tariffs throughout the world were started.

Phase IV - Quest for Identity (1956 - ?)

In 1956, Britain conducted the ill-fated Suez operation against Nasser and was opposed by the United States. As a result, Britain had to withdraw from the Middle East and this signalled a more general strategic retreat. Although billed as a military withdrawal of 'all points East of Suez', it signified a much more profound policy reorientation: the slow changing of the British Commonwealth from an 'Empire' to an 'Old Boys Club'. This left the Dominions of Canada and Australia more independent and forced to rely increasingly on their own capabilities. Britain, meanwhile, drew gradually closer to continental Europe, eventually joining the European Economic Community in the early seventies, after much hesitation. After that event, the British connection could no longer be counted-upon, in the economic sphere, to balance the influence of the United States. However, in the cultural field, Britain's influence continued to exert itself, while French Quebec sought increasing ties with France.

During the Diefenbaker era, in the late 1950s, the Conservatives adopted a strong nationalist anti-American and pro-European stance. At one point there was even a plan to divert 15 percent of Canada-United States trade towards Britain. In that period, it was once again the Liberals of Lester Pearson who advocated the rapprochement with the United States and the Conservatives of John Diefenbaker who defended the nationalist stance.

In fact, in the perspective of a century-old debate, the 1988 Liberal stance against free trade and the Conservative espousal of it appear as a historical anomaly - or a major break in long-term trends.

In the late sixties, Lester Pearson and Lyndon Johnson negotiated the Auto Pact, creating sectoral free trade in car parts between the two countries. This created the present pattern of bilateral trade with the United States exporting more to Ontario than to Japan, and Canada exporting $2.1 billion of auto parts to the United States in 1984. By that time, auto exports were the second leading Canadian export to the United States, after petroleum ($3.3

billion). On the U.S. side, automobile parts was the leading export to Canada ($19.8 billion), followed by industrial machinery ($5 billion).

Meanwhile, in Quebec, the Quiet Revolution took place and, ultimately, led to its modern version, the Independence movement. With the identity of Canada no longer as clear as it had been when it was a member of the once-powerful British Empire, centrifugal forces within the country increased their momentum.

In 1971, a weakening U.S. economy led to the swing of the pendulum back to protectionism in the United States and industrial strategies in Canada. Nixon's surcharge of 1971, along with his historic decision to end the post-war gold exchange standard, introduced an era of strong economic nationalism worldwide. The turbulence that followed was amplified by the two oil shocks of 1973 and 1979 and led to more state interventionism almost everywhere.

In Canada, the 1970s were marked by Canada's attempt to revive, in a new form, the European counterweight and to launch a nation-wide industrial strategy. The new version of the European counterweight was the 1974 Contractual Agreement between Canada and the European Economic Community. It was primarily motivated by the latest weakening of the British connection. 'Mother has remarried and we must make-do with the new reality' was the theme of the times. The new reality involved seeking a contractual link with the 'stepfather', the EEC, within which lived Canada's other 'mother' France and the mother-countries of many of its immigrants.

The Canada-European Economic Community Agreement, while never repealed, was never really consummated (in any meaningful sense), for two reasons. The first had to do with European attitudes towards Canada, which ranged from almost total ignorance to a perception of this country as a mere subset of the United States. The one notable exception was General de Gaulle who, as a veteran geopolitician, saw Canada's potential as an instrument in Europe's own search for a counterweight to 'le défi américain'. Heavily influenced by the journalist Claude Julien's book, *Le Canada, Dernière Chance de l'Europe*, he also strongly believed in the tradition of French mercantilism. By planned coincidence, when he came to visit Quebec for Expo 67, he arrived in a French cruiser appropriately called the *Colbert*. His attempt to revive Colbertism took root in an increasingly-separatist Quebec and gave international recognition and legitimacy to the movement which culminated in the creation of the Parti Québécois. Indeed, it was after the accolade given by de Gaulle to Quebec separatism in the form of his famous "Vive le Québec Libre" speech, that René Lévesque and other French Québécois personalities became involved in the movement.

The second reason for the failure of the Canada-European Economic Community Agreement was that Canadian businessmen, traditionally parochial and inward-looking, failed to identify meaningful opportunities in Europe - although these abounded and were seized by the Japanese and the Americans. On the whole, the agreement failed because the key players, the Canadian and European private sectors, refused to take each other seriously.

On the internal front, Canada's industrial strategy also floundered, for at least three reasons.

Firstly, Ottawa never 'got its act together'. As Richard French has pointed out, in his excellent book *How*

Ottawa Decides, the competition between the three centres of power within the federal government, the Department of Finance, Treasury Board and the Privy Council Office, ultimately neutralized the initiative. The proliferation of federal government departments with overlapping jurisdictions condemned the entire exercise to futility. Secondly, since federal-provincial relations were characterized by intense antagonism, each province decided to develop its own private industrial strategy to compete with, and sometimes neutralize, the federal one. Thirdly, Ottawa never succeeded in bringing 'on board' the private sector, which either sulked or clamoured for less government intervention. Many joint ventures between the private and public sectors failed miserably.

Although attempts at industrial strategies continued until 1984, and the defeat of the Liberals, they lost much of their steam in the early eighties when the mood towards the reduction of the state in economic matters became stronger.

When the Conservatives took power in 1984, the pendulum swung to the other side: free trade with the United States became the principal foreign policy objective and a decentralized Confederation emerged as the official internal priority. These new policy orientations resulted in the Meech Lake Accord in 1987 and the Free Trade Agreement with the United States in 1989.

The Hesitation Waltz in Perspective

The two centuries-long 'hesitation waltz' between Canada and the United States has had a number of common recurring elements which are eloquent indicators of the underlying ambivalence of both parties. As Figure 1 (page 66) shows, Canada has alternated between her three major external stances. The first stance, which we could call the American Option, involves an ever-closer rapprochement with the United States ranging, in principle, from sectoral free trade to complete political union. Canada has never answered this option with a full 'yes' or 'no', and instead has approached/avoided it with surprising regularity. Its periodic rejections of the American option have led Canada into playing out, in some combination or other, the second and third options: rebuilding from within as an internal counterweight, or relying on Europe as external counterweight.

As far as the American option is concerned, there have been no less than nine 'marriage proposals' since 1775. The first two were 'shotgun' proposals (1775, 1812) and the next seven, (1854, 1891, 1911, 1935-41, 1947, 1960s and 1987) limited economic partnerships, ranging in comprehensiveness from sectoral agreements like the Auto Pact to full reciprocity and the equivalent of a common market.

The recurring elements in the nine cases have been summarized by Earl Fry, Professor of Political Science and Chairman of Canadian Studies at Brigham Young University. They are:

1) Canada has usually been the petitioner, initiating the discussions, with the exception of the first two 'shotgun affairs', where Canada fought the United States (1775 and 1812).

2) The United States has consistently been 'cold to indifferent' on the subject of free trade with Canada, yet at times keenly interested in political integration, especially during the annexationist, Manifest Destiny stage.

3) In most of the cases, the negotiations were broken-off because Canada had a change of heart while they were in progress. This change of heart, typically, occurred on or

around a Canadian federal election, where the opposition party (against free trade) would be returned to power and would cancel the deal.

4) In those cases where an agreement was actually signed and implemented, the United States Congress changed its mind after a few years and abrogated the deal.

5) *Treaty or no treaty, Canada's economy has become, over the last two hundred years, inextricably integrated with that of the United States and increasingly disconnected from that of Europe. At every 'marriage proposal', certain irreversible steps were taken, drawing Canada closer to the United States.*

The overall pattern of hesitation is illustrated in Figure 1 below. The question is, what will happen in the future? Will the 'Hesitation Waltz' be extended into the nineties? There is every indication that it will, but there are also indications that this dance cannot continue indefinitely. In the first place, there is no longer an external counterweight. It must either be recreated or be replaced by other solutions. As for the internal counterweight, it is, at present, unclear and wrapped in ambiguity. Its future potential will be examined in the second part of the book. First, let us examine a missing part of the puzzle: what is happening in the larger global environment.

HISTORICAL PERIOD	FIRST OPTION RAPPROCHEMENT WITH THE UNITED STATES FROM FREE TRADE TO ULTIMATE POLITICAL UNION	SECOND OPTION REBUILDING FROM WITHIN: THE INTERNAL COUNTER-WEIGHT	THIRD OPTION THE EUOPEAN CONNECTION THE EXTERNAL COUNTER-WEIGHT
1600-1763	Competition with the British colonies. Periodic wars.	Incentives for population growth State interventionism	French mercantilist policies
1763-1812	War with the Thirteen Colonies Rejection of U.S. invitation to join Union. Anti-Americanism.	Religious tolerance	Military alliance with Britain Allegiance to the Crown
1813-1846	Resistance to United States annexationist pressures.	Some self-government	Economic alliance with Britain
1846-1866	Strong movement to join U.S. Reciprocity Treaty signed 1854	Bank on reciprocity	Allegiance to the Crown Repeal of the Corn Laws Weakening of European Link
1866-1891	Repeal of Reciprocity 1866 failure to revive it U.S. McKinley tariff	1867 Confederation National Policy: railway building and high external tariffs	European link becomes legal and ceremonial, and less economic Military guarantee of Canada given by Britain
1891-1911	Failure of 1911 Reciprocity 2 million Canadians migrate to the United States.		
1911-1930	Co-existence. Smoot-Hawley Tariff 1930	Normal government policies	Weakening of legal link with Britain; Statute of Westminster
1930-1947	3 Reciprocity Agreements signed by US/Canada. Some repealed.	Normal government policies	Weakening of economic links with Britain
1947-1984	Auto Pact with U.S. Anti-Americanism fuelled by Vietnam War.	Economic nationalism strong but ineffective. Provincial economic nationalism. Quebec separatism	Link with Britain and Europe weakens. Quebec link with France strengthened.
1984-1987	Free Trade with United States is priority objective. Free Trade Accord negotiated in 1987.	Decentralized Confederation is national priority. State-reduction policies instituted. Meech Lake Agreement, 1987.	European link is very weak. Now largely only ceremonial: i.e. the Monarchy and cultural ties.

Figure 1
The Canada/United States 'Hesitation Waltz'

Chapter 3

THE CHALLENGE OF GLOBALIZATION

It would be tempting at this stage to place the wide angle lens in a such a commanding position as to try and encompass 'everything' that has been happening in a sort of super, state-of-the-universe message. This temptation must be resisted on two grounds. First, 'state of the universe messages' are hard to come-by because of the complexity of the said universe. Second, not all trends have equal relevance to the subject at hand, which is where Canada fits in the global perspective. For this reason, we shall eschew a discussion of the dangers of nuclear war, the AIDS epidemic and hunger in Africa, all supremely important trends but which do not have more special effects on Canada than on anyone else.

There are, among contemporary currents of global change, five processes underway that have particular relevance for Canada. They are:
• The Third Industrial Revolution;
• The Globalization of Markets and Production;
• The Rise of the Pacific Rim;
• Europe 1992;
• The Threats and Opportunities Associated with the New World Order.

The Third Industrial Revolution.

Since about 1945, the world has been experiencing what should properly be called a 'third industrial revolution'. The first industrial revolution took place in the period 1750 - 1870. A key innovation, the steam engine, engendered a series of complementary innovations and propelled Britain to worldwide industrial dominance. British products out-competed those of everyone else and their export supported the *Pax Britannica*. Gradually the rest of the world adopted British innovations and improved on them, and by 1870, about a dozen countries were 'industrialized': their principal economic activity was now technology-intensive manufacturing, rather than resource-intensive agriculture.

The second industrial revolution occurred in the period from about 1870 to the end of the Second World War. It featured three major innovations and a series of minor ones. The first of these three was electricity - not a source but a form of energy that could be transmitted over long distances. Large countries like Canada could then enter the industrial race by harnessing their electrical potential. Electricity also introduced enormous flexibility in the use of energy, which could now be employed to heat or cool, to propel, to light, to transport and to communicate. The electrical revolution developed slowly but steadily and set the stage for follow-up revolutions, notably the electronic. The second major industrial innovation of the period 1870-1945 was the piston, or internal combustion, engine. This led to the development of the automobile, the truck and ultimately the airplane. The third and final major innovation of this period was steel, which replaced iron as the industrial material of choice for all heavy-duty applications.

The second industrial revolution of 1870-1945 witnessed the relative decline of Britain as a world power and the emergence of the United States and Germany. Germany missed its chance by being defeated in two World Wars, but the United States established its pre-eminence and became *the* world superpower in 1945.

After 1945, the pace of innovation reached a new crescendo. As in the case of the previous two industrial revolutions, the third one started-out with a major innovation in the energy field - nuclear power. However, the environmental disruption associated with the use of that form of energy led to its limited dissemination as a source of power - much more limited than was originally envisioned by the scientists and politicians of the forties and fifties.

The third industrial revolution became more a revolution in information than in energy technologies. This led to the current 'information economies' - economies whose principal economic activity is the processing of information rather than of energy and materials. The ferment of the revolution in information technologies saw computers developed through four generations, achieving the very high rate of penetration we now witness in all aspects of our lives. A fifth generation is currently under development which claims to be able to produce 'artificial intelligence'. Allied to this computer revolution has been a telecommunication revolution, featuring digital telephony, cable distribution, satellite transmissions, fibre optics and interactive television.

Because of the all-encompassing nature of the information revolution, a number of additional generic or 'structural' technologies have since developed. These include biotechnology, superconductors and new synthetic materials. In addition, continuing improvements in energy, transportation and communication are feeding the innovation process, which today has achieved exponential proportions.

The acceleration of the rate of change of technological innovation and the overnight penetration of new technologies into hitherto unlikely areas is creating a very dynamic and volatile world economy, where winners and losers can be made or destroyed overnight. Therefore, any consideration of the global 'big picture' must assign to technology its proper place: *For good or for ill, technological change is probably now the single most influential factor in shaping our future.*

The Globalization of Markets and Production.

One of the consequences of the technological change that has occurred in the last forty years in transportation, communication, energy and computers has been to make factors of production, previously immobile across international borders, now quite 'footloose' on a global scale.

Economic theory distinguishes between four categories of productive agents: natural resources, capital, labour and technology. All four are, today, much more mobile across international boundaries than they were a century ago. In particular, capital and technology can roam across the earth's surface and settle in the most unlikely places. As Peter Drucker has pointed out,in a 1986 article in *Foreign Affairs* , capital movements are a much more significant part of the international economy than international trade. The 'symbol' economy has replaced the 'real' economy. In 1986, world trade amounted to about $2.5 to $3 trillion, while the London Euro-dollar market alone posted $75 trillion-worth of international transactions.

The global mobility, not only of capital and technology, but to a lesser extent of labour and of resources, has led to an international economy where competitive advantage is not fixed but shifting. Since competitive advantage is the result of particular factor endowments within each country, as these endowments change with trans-national factor mobility, competitive advantage shifts with them. What this means is that factories established in Nova Scotia may move overnight to Mexico to operate in another subsidiary of the multinational. This is the threat. The opportunity comes from the possibility of the reverse process: factories established in Mexico (or California, Wisconsin or Italy) moving to Nova Scotia.

The globalization of markets and production means that all the world has become one economic entity. The economic trend is towards globalization, but the political trend is towards smaller regional entities, such as continents. There is, therefore, a potential structural opposition between globalization, which breaks down international barriers, and continentalism which, on the contrary, creates new ones. *Canada, in the nineties, will have to decide whether it will play the global or the continental card.*

The Rise of the Pacific Rim

One of the consequences of international factor mobility has been a gradual shift of the centre of world economic power from the Atlantic to the Pacific. The United States and Europe, the two pillars of the Atlantic economy, with Canada 'between them' in a geopolitical sense, are now being ousted from pre-eminence by the Southeast Asian Triangle composed of Japan, the 'Mini-Dragons' (Hong-Kong, South Korea, Singapore and Taiwan) and China.

Whether this shift is permanent or reversible is not clear at this time. What is clear is that a relative decline of the United States has occurred since 1945, the year which marked the apex of U.S. power.   The U.S. decline has been primarily economic.   However, as in the case of the Soviet Union, economic decline has been masked by military build-ups.   In addition, unlike in the Soviet Union, decline in the United States has also been masked by heavy borrowing from abroad and 'paper entrepreneurship': astute financial operations on the stock market that add nothing to the economy but make instant millionaires out of particularly adept speculators.

   During the Reagan presidency, 1980-1988, the United States vaulted back from the apparent decline in military and geopolitical prestige of the Carter years to a semblance of recovery.   The 1984 Olympic Games in Los Angeles revealed a confident United States in both the sports and the economic arenas.   America's military build-up was frightening the Russians, her economy was vanquishing inflation and experimenting with supply side economics, and foreign investment came in from everywhere.   High real interest rates bolstered the value of the dollar, which reached unprecedented heights in 1985 against the yen and all other currencies.   Following the severe recession of 1981-1982, the recovery of 1983 led to the longest bull market in history, when the Dow Jones climbed to dizzying summits.   The money illusion which resulted from this bull market led some observers to believe that the long-term trend of U.S. decline had been reversed.

   This proved to be false.   The recovery of 1983-89 in the United States was fuelled by outside capital, mainly Japanese, investing heavily in the U.S. stock market and financing U.S. consumption habits.   It was also stimulated by the simplest of Keynesian mechanisms, government spending legitimized as military expenditures. During this period, the United States moved from the position of major-creditor to major-debtor nation externally and internally, amassing record fiscal deficits. These twin towers of debt were further financed by foreign borrowing and an overvalued U.S. dollar. After 1985, the trend was reversed and the U.S. dollar started to plummet. Between February 1985 and December 1987, it plunged from an equivalent of 250 to 120 yen. In addition, on October 19, 1987, the world stock markets crashed, thus signalling the beginning of possible strong turbulence on world financial markets.

Above and beyond the paper entrepreneurship charade, U.S. decline manifested itself in four ways. First and foremost was a softening of the U.S. industrial base: a gradual de-industrialization of the economy and the transformation of the old smokestack factories into a gigantic 'rust belt'. Secondly, the American consumption ethos, heavily in favour of 'now' over 'tomorrow' spending, strengthened by the 'Yuppie' ideology and the climbing Dow Jones, led to a massive increase in *private borrowing* and added a third tower of debt to the economic picture. Now there were three deficits - that of the U.S. government, that of the American consumers, and the foreign debt that resulted from the first two. Thirdly, international factor mobility and the changes brought about by the third industrial revolution led to continuing migration of production to Southeast Asia and away from the United States. Fourthly and finally, the U.S. seemed at a loss to explain what, in fact, was happening and failed to propose viable long-term solutions beyond the bull market.

The rise of Japan has been the symmetrical opposite to U.S. decline. From a weak base at the end of

World War II, Japan has emerged as an economic superpower, penetrating sector after sector of international economic activity and generally becoming the best at whatever it tried to do. In the wake of its success have come the 'Mini-Dragons' of Southeast Asia, each imitating the Japanese pattern, and in some cases even leap-frogging Japan itself. And behind them all lies the might of China, the sleeping giant, whose awakening may be as traumatic to Japan as it is to the West.

Whether the future holds a Japanese- or Chinese-dominated Asia Pacific region cannot yet be predicted, but what is already clear is that if present trends are not reversed, *world economic leadership will shift from the Atlantic to the Pacific by the end of the century.* Events may, of course, change. Trend is not 'destiny'. But long-term processes will not change automatically. New conditions have to be met, for some trends to be reversed. We will examine what these are in the second part of this book, but for now let us note the handwriting on the wall: *there will be a declining United States of America in the international arena, and a more dominant United States on the North American continent,* at least as far as Canada is concerned.

Europe 1992

The other major partner of Canada is, of course, Europe. For all intents and purposes, Europe has been following the same trajectory as the United States: gradual de-industrialization and the loss of competitive advantage in favour of Southeast Asia. Europe retains, however, a number of high cards. First, it harbours a few 'Japans' of its own. It has a 'former Japan' in Britain, since that country managed to be the workshop of the world for a century and a half. It also has 'Japan' cousins in West Germany, Austria and Switzerland, and possible future 'Japans' in France and Italy. The industrial and technological potential is there and so are the natural and human resources.

In addition, Europe has the EEC, the most extensive economic and political bloc in the world. The EEC is the first trading region in the world and its combined GNP by far the highest in the world. If the EEC were united in one country, it would be the most powerful country in the world, dwarfing both the United States and Japan and outdistancing the Soviet Union. But it is not yet politically-united, and may or may not ever fully become so. Its drive for unity has been externally-motivated through fear of the Soviet Union. It sought, in collective security and the Common Market, its own internal counterweight to the Soviet threat. Like Canada, it also sought an external counterweight in the United States and its nuclear umbrella. But the process of its political unification is painfully slow.

The watershed year is likely to be 1992. According to present plans, this year should mark the elimination of all tariff and non-tariff barriers to internal European trade. By the end of the century, if '1992' follows its agenda, a European political confederation may be in the works. Already, on many issues, Europe has a common external policy. Its unification may extend to many other fields.

If Europe were indeed to complete its unification process and look outward, it would exert considerable gravitational pull across the Atlantic and reactivate the counterweight role it played for Canada in North America. *Alternatively, a federal Europe which would be inward looking would drive Canada much further into the arms of the United States.* In both cases, what happens to Europe in the next twelve years will be very important for Canada. A disunited or a strongly-introverted Europe would strengthen the American Option for Canada, while an extroverted, united Europe would draw Canada closer. A plausible longer-term option would then be a new Atlantic common market, including the United States, Europe and the EEC as a symmetrical counterweight to the Southeast Asian triangle.

The Threats and Opportunities Associated with the New World Order

Contemporary processes of global change have brought with them high 'turbulence'. They are not smooth and gradual but sometimes sudden and discrete. The pace of change has been accelerating and the turbulence which it involves is not necessarily negative. It is, as the economist Schumpeter once put it, a process of "creative destruction." The old order is being replaced by a new one and there are winners and losers.

The old order was the "Pax Americana", which functioned relatively flawlessly from 1945 to about 1971. It rested on three pillars: the military predominance of the United States; its industrial supremacy; and the Bretton Woods international monetary system, which maintained a gold exchange standard that actually was a U.S. dollar standard.

As far as military predominance is concerned, the world is now much closer to a bi-polar stalemate than it was in 1971, when the gap between the two superpowers was significantly in favour of the United States.

As far as industrial supremacy is concerned, the two oil shocks and the rise of Southeast Asia challenged the old industrial order and raised the spectre of 'de-industrialization', a term hitherto unknown. De-industrialization meant that a country that had managed to industrialize successfully and had a thriving manufacturing-base could become de-industrialized and lose that base to foreign competition. Britain showed it could be done. The first country to industrialize was also the first to de-industrialize. British cars, for instance, once the pride of the industry, gradually disappeared from the market place - not only the international market place, but the British one as well. What happened to Britain in the seventies and eighties may be an indicator of things to come.

Finally, as far as Bretton Woods is concerned, the decision of the United States to resort to flexible exchange rates and a U.S. dollar no longer tied to gold, freed the international exchanges, but at the same time introduced great uncertainties into the system.

The widely fluctuating exchange rates became threats to the stability of international trade and led to increased capital movements, some clearly destabilizing. Short-term capital began chasing rising currencies and distorted the international investment picture by introducing casino-style strategies to an otherwise very serious area of economic activity. The net result was a boom and bust cycle exemplified by the year 1987, which boasted the five highest single-day gains of the Dow Jones in history, accompanied by the five steepest single-day losses! The most abrupt single-day fall of 1987 occurred on "Meltdown Monday", October 19, when the Dow Jones plummeted for 22 percent of its value, as opposed to the 'mere' 12 percent loss, which occurred in the Great Crash of 1929.

In sum, at the dawn of the nineties, the global system is undergoing profound changes. These changes bring with them a certain number of threats, and perhaps an even greater number of opportunities - for the stout-hearted. The process of creative destruction, brought about by rapid technological change, is creating winners and losers. Interestingly, in this global competition, winning and losing is not a 'one time' thing. On the contrary, global turbulence is breeding a class of habitual winners and, sadly, a counterpart-class of habitual losers. *This is because comparative advantage has shifted from products to processes.* The Japanese have shown that it is possible to be good not only at a handful of things but at almost everything, if productive processes are fully mastered. It follows that the opportunities awaiting innovative entrepreneurs are immense.

Where does that leave Canada? Between Continentalism and a Global Strategy, Canada has enormous potential. The country is in excellent field position to make good use of global opportunities once it has put its house in order. But is the house in order? This is the question to which we now turn.

PART II

HOW CANADA?

... Unlocking the Handbrake ...

We have shown, in the last three chapters, that the question "Why Canada?" will become increasingly meaningful as the 1990s unfold. We have argued that good answers to this question will be essential if Canada wants an alternative to what we have called a "Continental Destiny." Related to the question of "Why?" is the question of "How?". Which design of the Canadian federation will permit itbest to meet its challenges, and how far is the existing framework a help, or a hindrance?

To tackle this question we proceed, in Part II, first by assessing Canada's comparative performance in the concert of nations. The review is mixed. In absolute terms, Canada has done well and has positioned itself, in many areas, among the first ten nations on earth. But compared to the achievements Canada's immense potential could support, this performance is unsatisfactory. In fact, Canada is too obsessed with 'middleness' and too easily satisfied with bronze medals, even when gold are definitely within grasp. The unambitious objectives, that the country so often places on its agenda, become self-fulfilling prophecies. Overall, the performance is good but falls far short of the excellence this nation, with its rich natural and human endowments, is capable of achieving.

There are, in our view, two principal reasons for this less-than-superlative performance. The first is what we have called Canada's *"National Adversary System "*. Although based on the laudable principle of checks and balances (itself imported from the British parliamentary system), Canada's operating style is that of systematic adversarial relations, masquerading as high democracy. Its basic premise is that only by opposition can organizations be kept in check. From Her Majesty's 'loyal opposition' in Ottawa, to federal/provincial squabbling over almost everything, Canada has, inadvertently, put in place a locked handbrake which stymies initiative and which slows progress - in spite of the powerful potential of the national engine.

At least four major adversary systems dominate Canadian society.   The first and most visible is *Federal/Provincial Confrontation* where decisions are made following an auction model that sees the noisiest partner getting most of the goodies. The second is the *Public Sector vs Private Sector Mode of Mutual Distrust* . In spite of the existence of a large number of Crown corporations and para-public sector enterprises, the public/private interface has never been fully thought-out, with adverse results. Unlike some of today's winners, like Japan and West Germany, who excel in public/private synergy and concerted action, Canada maintains, instead, an opposition mode. The third is the *Labor/Management Confrontation,* quite severe in the seventies, somewhat less severe in the eighties, but possibly returning in strength in the nineties. The fourth is the prevalence of *Small Firm vs. Small Firm Competition,* which is encouraged by Canada's laws and fiscal regulation. Again, although based on the very legitimate principle of protecting the consumer by discouraging bigness, this kind of competition has the negative effect of reducing Canada's ability to achieve world-class product mandates against the major foreign multinationals.

The second major reason why bronze and not gold is achieved is Canada's lack of a clear *mission statement* or a galvanizing *projet de société* that could mobilize the masses and harness the nation's vital energies. Instead, the country's identity remains ambiguous and diffuse and is torn between two competing nationalisms, a strong and vibrant Quebec nationalism and a much weaker, more ambivalent Canadian version, often confused with Ontarian provincialism. If 'mission statements' and 'corporate culture' are key ingredients in the quest for excellence of private sector firms, they are even more important at the nation-state level - especially when geopolitical forces constantly challenge Canada's raison d'être.

In Part II then, we examine the evolution of the four adversarial relations and the problem of the mission statement, and outline the possible outcomes in the nineties. The overall thesis is simple: Canada has probably the next decade to get its act together - but not much longer!

Chapter 4

BRONZEMANIA!... OR THE CULT OF 'MIDDLENESS'!

A Passion for Bronze.
At the beginning of the twentieth century, Canada and Argentina were considered by some knowledgeable observers to be emerging global superpowers, not necessarily in a quantitative sense, but in the more subtle sense of the 'pursuit of excellence'. Arnold Toynbee argued that the century would ultimately belong to the French Canadians, while others felt that Argentina's immense resources and potential would make that country into *the* model nation. In 1900, the United States was already a great power, Russia a sleeping giant, China a source of great anxiety (the "Yellow Peril") and Japan still taken rather lightly by the West, in spite of the Meiji revolution. Now, towards the end of the twentieth century, how does the balance sheet read?

The United States is still, at the dawn of the nineties, the number-one global power, with Japan challenging very closely and, according to some observers, poised to surpass our southern neighbour very soon. Britain, the premier power of 1900, is in the throes of involuntary de-industrialization and relative decline, although the British economy rebounded in the mid-1980s. Whether this rebound is a 'flash in the pan' or the beginning of a renaissance is unclear. The prognosis for one of Canada's mother-countries is still mixed. Indeed, after a century of ruling 'the waves' and the international economy too, Britannia has relinquished world power. The process of decline may have started as early as 1870, becoming visible only a century later, in the 1960s. Germany is still split in two (though recent events may lead to unification); however, both halves maintain a tradition of excellence in many sectors. Their economic strength would justify a much louder voice in world affairs, but the sequels of the Second World War have forced that country to tread softly and maintain a low political profile - although this attitude may not last much longer. France is doing much better, overall, than would have been expected, especially compared with Britain yet it, too, is in the throes of powerful turbulence, as is most of Western Europe.

Within the European context, special mention must be made of four other countries. Switzerland has, of course, been a perennial model of a small country showing how selective excellence can be made profitable and lasting. Austria has, to some extent, followed a similar path. A 'sick man of Europe' at the time of the Austro-Hungarian Empire, Austria has managed, since the late 1950s, to a carve itself a niche by 'piggy-backing' on Germany. It has managed, however, not to become dominated by its more powerful neighbour, and this has prompted some observers to point to the Austrian example as a good model for Canada. Sweden remains a model of a mixed economy, very socialist according to some indicators, and extremely capitalist according to others. Finally, since the mid-eighties, Italy has been the most interesting success story, leading some observers to talk about an Italian 'miracle'. What is striking about the Italian case is that that country's success has been achieved in spite of unstable and changing governments. A strong, informal economy with a pattern of underground, non-market mediated economic transactions, seems to be a key to Italy's success. This experience, too, may be a model for Canada.

What of Argentina and Canada? Interestingly, these two countries have much in common. They both have populations of about 25 million, principally of European descent, and occupy the extremities of their respective continents. Both enjoy very generous endowments of natural resources and are flanked by more populous, more dynamic immediate neighbours, Brazil and the United States respectively. These immediate neighbours seem to cause structural anxiety in the psyche of each country. Argentina fears Brazil and yet grudgingly admires its better performance. Canada has an approach-avoidance relationship with the United States that has lasted for over two centuries. In both cases, the foreign outlooks of Argentina and of Canada are strongly conditioned by their relationships with their two strong neighbours.

Argentina has not lived up to expectations. Its Achilles heel has been an inability to achieve the social consensus necessary to the successful pursuit of excellence. A well-known joke in Argentinean circles is to report that "God the Father gave Argentina everything - a wonderful landscape, fertile land, mineral resources, a clement climate and then, feeling he had given too much, decided to saddle the country with... Argentineans!" The free-for-all, built-in adversary system, which has characterized Argentinean politics and economics for the last seventy-five years has been its undoing. Argentina has not realized its potential and is unlikely to do so without profound structural change. Successive coups d'état and revolutions have attempted to bring about that needed structural change, without any great success so far.

Perhaps the return to civilian rule in 1984 will prove to have been the beginning of a fuller development for Argentina. Time will tell.

Canada has performed much better than Argentina. In an absolute sense it has done well, and is ranked among the rich and lucky nations of this earth. The international perception of Canada abroad is positive. In surveys done

---

CANADA'S RESOURCE ENDOWMENT IN IMPORTANT MINERALS
Percentage Share of World Mineral Resources

	Canada	World Rank in 1981
Asbestos	35.6%	1
Bismuth	15.8	2
Columbium	3.5	2
Copper	6.3	5
Gypsum	10.3	2
Ilmenite	25.2	1
Iron Ore	8.5	5
Lead	13.3	4
Molybdenum	6.6	4
Potash	68.7	1
Silver	19.0	3
Sulphur	11.0	1
Tantalum	8.3	4
Tungsten	14.8	2
Zinc	26.8	1

Source: U.S Bureau of Mines, *Commodity Summaries*, Washington D.C and U.S Department of Interior adapted from P. Caragata, *Natural Resources and International Bargaining Power,* (Kingston: Queen's University Press, 1984), 136.

Figure 2.

before the Versailles Western summit in the mid-eighties, Canada was singled-out as the most desirable country by European respondents who were asked to list the next best country after their own. But there is ambivalence. Many foreign observers feel that, given its assets, Canada should do much better. As one Canadian pension manager of European descent put it, "there are two views of Canada in Europe".

The first we can attribute to a fictional Frenchman, "Jean-Jacques" who views Canada as an ideal haven for investment and perhaps ultimately as his principal residence. Canada's high political stability is praised and, in this sense, it is in marked contrast with the instability of the Third World and even that of Europe. Its pleasant cultural environment and relatively safe streets also make it a highly desirable nation.

However, opposing "Jean-Jacques'" view, is the more severe assessment by a German businessman, "Klaus-Peter" (or for that matter "Kyuzo" from Japan, "Chuck" from the United States or "Kim" from Korea). They believe that the Canadian economy is somehow mismanaged and that there is a lack of creativeness and innovative entrepreneurship in the country. The quality of the labour force is given mixed ratings and the country, as a whole, viewed as a backwater region. In fact, there is a distinct feeling in some circles that, in spite of its natural endowment and human resources, the country is not a 'winner'.

Although superbly endowed, Canada has produced, overall, a distinctly middling performance. The cult of 'middleness' has permeated the national character. Canada is supposed to be a 'middle' power with 'middle' ambitions and a 'middle' identity. Consequently, it can only expect of

itself mediocre results! This frame of mind is illustrated by
the joy we often express at obtaining the bronze medal in
international competition. Going for the bronze has been
the acceptable thing to do, just as attaining a "C" grade is
the acceptable thing for a 'Gentleman'. To try for the gold
is considered presumptuous and perhaps even
undemocratic. In the convoluted and heroic apologies we
have made for the 'middle road' we have also invented new
performance indicators. In the Calgary Winter Olympic
Games of 1988, Canada obtained no gold medals and only
managed a few bronze. Even in hockey, Canada's gift to
the world of sport, we did not make the medal round,
although we were superbly equipped to do so. Perhaps the
ultimate rationalization of the cult of middleness was made
when a group of journalists tried to devise an indicator of
number of finishes *in the first eight..* That index did
indeed show a reasonably good performance for Canada -
if that is what we are looking for. But is a middling
existence what the country should openly strive for?

To be sure, middleness has not been uncomfortable
and, for this reason, it is very viable. Canada's immense
cushion of natural resources prevents mediocrity from
degenerating into absolute decline. Barring natural
diasters, nature's heritage allows for a *rentier* existence:
living off the fat of the land. True, the winters are long but
when the spring comes the land is rich and we are not
likely to run out of apples, wheat, petroleum, pulp, paper
and electricity. Therefore, why try harder? *In its constant
search for the Olympic bronze, even when gold was within
its grasp, Canada has pursued a path far short of its
capabilities.* Its situation is similar to that of a hockey
superstar content with a twenty-goal season. Now a
twenty-goal season is respectable and above average but it

is, nevertheless, not outstanding and cannot compare with a fifty-goal season.

The Potential for Gold

The odds against a child being born in Canada, rather than in Ethiopia, the Andes or Bangladesh are very high. Therefore, those of us who were born here or who have emigrated to this country may consider ourselves lottery winners in the great sweepstakes of the human condition. We are hardly aware of this and seem not at all inclined to use, to their fullest extent, the wild cards that nature has dealt us.

Canada's principal comparative advantage is, of course, rooted in its magnificent resource endowment. In this sense it is a polar opposite of Japan. Whereas Japan has to import virtually all the raw materials it needs for its economic livelihood, Canada is either self-sufficient in or a net exporter of most of them.

When a country has to import 100 percent of its aluminium, 99 percent of its oil, 98 percent of its iron ore and 66 percent of its wood and lumber, like Japan does, it has no alternative but to try harder. Without competitiveness, the Japanese economy would be condemned to sink into the ocean. There are no safety nets. In contrast, the Canadian economy can afford to be wasteful. With only 25 million people living off the second largest country in the world, we are the least likely to run out of raw materials.

In energy and food, Canada is a net exporter. If Canada suffered during the energy crisis of the seventies, it was due to inappropriate energy policies, and to federal-provincial and provincial-provincial rivalries. One remembers the slogan of some irate Western Canadians,

"Let the Eastern bastards freeze in the dark." Whereas other countries had to struggle to export commodities in order to pay for oil imports, Canada had to import oil partially because of the absence of appropriate transportation modes for Western oil. Overall there are few OECD countries better endowed than Canada in food and in oil - key strategic raw materials. As far as minerals are concerned, as Figure 2 shows, Canada rates a first in the world for asbestos, ilmenite, potash, sulphur and zinc, a second in four other key minerals and no worse than fifth place for the next six. There is no shortage of minerals in this country.

Canada's scientific and technological potential is also very high. This country has been a leader in transportation and telecommunication technology, and Canadian scientists have distinguished themselves in many fields of pure research. Overall, the people in this country are among the best trained and most competent in the world. Our human potential has been constantly enriched by a steady flow of immigrants from the Old World and the Third World, as well as from the Americas.

The general competitive picture is potentially excellent. Repeated surveys in the early and late eighties have ranked Canada from sixth to ninth in global competitiveness. In 1984, Canada was judged to be first in natural endowment, third in financial dynamism, fifth in human resources and sixth in market dynamics. However, it was also judged to be eleventh in entrepreneurial dynamism, fourteenth in industrial efficiency, fourteenth in socio-political consensus and sixteenth in terms of state interference in the economy. In most of the comparisons, the countries ahead of Canada were the United States, Switzerland, Japan, Germany, Denmark and Sweden.

With all its assets, it is a wonder that Canada is not at the top of the list in economic performance. One cannot help wondering what the Japanese could do if they controlled an equivalent natural endowment, since they seem to be doing so well with almost nothing. Why then has Canadian performance not been superlative?

Centrifugal versus Centralizing Forces.

Canada's geopolitical predicament, described in Chapter 2, has created two major challenges that have conditioned Canada's history: the external one which was and is the immense gravitational pull of the United States, and the internal one which consists of strong centrifugal forces pulling away in different directions. These centrifugal forces have been kept in check by a number of centralizing policies, and it is the perennial struggle between these two that makes up Canada's internal reality. This struggle is also, in our view, at the root of Canada's apparent inability to 'go for the gold' and fully realize its potential as a nation.

What are the centrifugal forces and how do they express themselves? They fall, in fact, into five groups: regionalism, provincialism, ethnic diversity, urban-rural splits and political ideology.

Regionalism exists when perceptions of reality and the organization of interest groups are determined by geographical territory. Distance combines with the uneven distribution of population in this enormous land to make regional identification very strong in Canada. The West sees Central Canada as a monolithic force whose interests are diametrically opposed to its own. Westerners frequently talk about an alleged Ontario-Quebec conspiracy aimed at keeping the Western provinces down.

This perception was even stronger during the Trudeau years, when federal policies were viewed with great distrust. One extreme Westerner even argued that the introduction of the metric system was a Central Canadian plot to subjugate the West. Central Canada, on the other hand, does not see itself as united and the Ontario-Quebec opposition, on many issues, is testimony to that lack of unity. The Maritime provinces tend to be suspicious both of the West and of Central Canada and there is a definite cleavage between the perceived interests of the Northern Territories and those of Southern Canada.

Regionalism is fed by unequal growth patterns. In the seventies, the Western provinces expanded, Quebec and the Maritimes contracted and Ontario prospered. In 1982-86, Central Canada expanded, the West and the Maritimes contracted and Ontario prospered. On the economic front, the federal government must consider at least two Canadas when it makes public policy: central Canada and the peripheral provinces. The scale of the game makes for very big winners and very big losers. This is why a central axiom of Canadian economic policy has always been to look at the regional implications of whatever policy instrument is chosen to deal with a particular problem. Without regional policies, the natural trend would be towards excessive concentration in Ontario and to a lesser extent Quebec, with but 'crumbs' left for the rest of the country.

Regionalism also spawns sub-regionalism. There is a natural tendency in British Columbia to view the Rockies as an important psychological barrier and to seek affinities with California further south or the Asian Pacific Rim further west. The Prairie provinces are marked by some similarities, but also by major differences. During the oil boom of the seventies, unequal resource endowment among the Prairie provinces placed Alberta in a class by itself. Ontario and Quebec are very different in their likes, dislikes and ways of life. The Maritimes have some homogeneity, but exhibit major differences too. Newfoundland considers itself an Atlantic rather than a Maritime Province and has separate interests. In fact, Newfoundlanders continue to call the mainland "Canada" as if they were not fully part of it.

Ultimately, the imperative of distance also creates micro-regionalism where 'home' is defined in a very restricted sense. Thus, one English Canadian claimed that he considered himself a 'citizen of Algoma' - a sub-region of Ontario - rather than of Canada. Maritimers in cities like St. John, Fredericton, Moncton and Charlottetown sometimes perceive as their greatest enemy, not Central Canada or Ontario or Quebec or Toronto or Montreal but ... Halifax. Halifax is viewed as the great centralizer, the drain which saps human resources away from the rest of the Maritimes. In Quebec, many new Canadians identify emotionally neither with Canada nor with their province, but with their city, Montreal. Some devoted Montrealers would gladly fight for a city-state and feel only mild attachment to larger entities. In Winnipeg, the emotional identification of its residents is said to be based on which part of Winnipeg one comes from.

The forces of regionalism find some expression quite naturally in provincialism, which may be defined as nationalism at the provincial level. Quebec has a strong national identity at the provincial level and, to some extent, so do Alberta, British Columbia, Ontario and Newfoundland. The ten provincial premiers are a major force to be reckoned with in Canada, since the Canadian

Constitution, both by design and by custom, gives strong powers to the provincial governments (greater powers to tax and spend than American states have, for example).

This means that every province can, and does, create its own political and economic reality, juxtaposing it upon the federal reality. All provinces have major ministries with names similar to their federal counterparts (Industry and Commerce, Technology, Culture, Health, Manpower, even Immigration). What this means is that there are considerable areas of overlap and, therefore, of potential friction between the two levels of government.

When John A. Macdonald created his National Policy to reinforce the economic unity of the country, he enjoyed, as head of the federal government, more relative power than when Pierre Trudeau attempted his 'industrial strategy'. Trudeau's industrial strategy had to contend with ten others. When there are eleven different strategies, each trying to do the same things, the result may be total cancellation of effort and little net output. Even as recently as 1988, while the debate about free trade with the United States raged on, the deeper debate about interprovincial trade barriers was largely ignored. In the strict sense of the term, trade within Canada is not free. It is encumbered by restrictive and protectionist provincial policies that often tend to cancel each other out.

Beyond regionalism and provincialism, <u>ethnic diversity</u> exerts an additional centrifugal tug at the body politic - although it has the potential to become a very strong unifying force, as will be argued elsewhere. Ethnic diversity, in its simplest form, takes shape in the 'two solitudes', the French-speaking Québecois versus the English-speaking Canadians of English, Scottish and Irish descent. With time, these much celebrated original solitudes have gone forth and multiplied. First, the legitimate aspirations of the native peoples of Canada, (themselves far from a homogeneous group), have begun to surface and the same character of 'distinctness', now recognized for the two founding nations, may one day also be given to the native people. The two solitudes will have become at least three. But the process is unlikely to stop there. The Ukrainian immigrant to the Prairies, the Greek, Italian or Portuguese immigrant to Quebec, or the Chinese and Pakistani immigrants to Ontario will not necessarily assimilate into any of the above three solitudes, but quite possibly will form their own. *Thus, there is a distinct danger of maximizing solitudes under the guise of diversity.*

An additional source of division is the urban-rural split that is much more characteristic of Canada than of the United States. Canadians are much more urbanized than Americans (and, some say, more urbane!). Twenty-nine percent of Canadians live in metropolitan areas of over one million (Toronto, Montreal, Vancouver) as against 8 percent in the United States. Fifty-six percent of Canadians live in cities and towns over 100,000, compared to 25 percent in the States. This strengthens the co-existence of two parallel lifestyles, a rural small-town lifestyle and an urban one with its different values and preferences (Gwyn, *The 49th Paradox*, p. 181).

A last centrifugal element is geographically-conditioned difference in political ideology. For much of the seventies and part of the eighties, Canada voted in regional blocs: the West shut out the Liberals and Quebec shut out the Conservatives and the New Democrats. The pattern was changed in the 1984 federal election, but the general trend of regionally-based bloc voting remains a feature of the Canadian body politic. In the 1988 federal election, regional bloc voting occurred in Quebec, Alberta, British Columbia and the Maritimes, with the rest of the country splitting down the middle over the free trade issue.

Against this array of centrifugal forces three opposing centralizing forces have arisen over time: fear of the United States, fear of Quebec separation, and fear of outside competitors.

Fear of the United States has been the traditional potion for national unity. It led to Confederation, to the National Policy of high tariffs and country-building, to industrial strategies, to an interventionist federal government in the Trudeau era and to the CRTC. It remains a rallying cry which will sometimes bring the entire country together. Fear of Quebec separation has also been a traditional centralizing force. In the seventies, when the threat of Quebec separation was clear and immediate, the country rallied around the flag to attempt to roll back separatist forces and design a new co-operative federalism. This led to the patriation of the Constitution, in 1981, and to the negotiation of the Meech Lake Accord in 1987. Finally, fear of outside competitors, rendered more imminent by the globalization of markets, is paving the way to some consensus on national economic policy.

Canada's National Adversary System.

The conflict between the centrifugal and centralizing forces in Canada has shaped the country's present political-economic system, which we characterize here as Canada's National Adversary System. Adversarial relations are the modus operandi and the underlying philosophy of legitimate conflict finds expression in four major adversary systems. These may be described as follows: Federal versus Provincial, Public sector versus Private sector, Labour versus Management and Firm versus Firm.

The most visible adversary system resides within the public sector of Canada and opposes the two levels of government, the central or federal on the one hand and the provincial on the other. The arena of conflict arises from the legal ambivalence of the Canadian Constitution and the vague interpretation of areas of jurisdiction. Since Canada is a confederation rather than a true federation, sovereignty, or the ultimate decision-making power, is shared between the central government and the provinces. As a result, a built-in opposition characterizes inter-governmental relations within the public sector.

With the passage of time, more adversarial relations are developing. The municipal level of government is becoming more autonomous. Some even argue that large cities like Montreal, Toronto, Vancouver, Halifax, Calgary, should each be represented abroad in a para-diplomatic mode and compete with each other for international investment. Already, inter-municipal rivalry is extremely strong. Many municipalities in the Greater Montreal region act as if they are in a death-struggle one with the others. Thus, Chateauguay, Laval, St. Laurent, and the South Shore all compete for the same 'goodies': industrial parks, convention halls, high-tech centres, and so on. In the Maritimes, the competition between Halifax and Moncton is intense, while in Alberta the Edmonton/ Calgary duel captures the popular imagination. The inter-municipal conflict 'piggy-backs' on an interprovincial one which is even more acute. The Ontario-Quebec rivalry, for instance, is now proverbial. In November 1988, the best way to sell free trade to some Quebecers was to show that it was bad for Ontario!

More minor, but nevertheless significant, adversary systems continue to emerge. Within a given level of government, especially the federal, inter-departmental rivalry is very strong and the 'protection of turfs' becomes a leading motivator for ministerial policies. Even within individual departments, inter-branch adversarial relations are strong.

The second most visible adversary system pits the public against the private sector. Governments in Canada, whether federal or provincial, tend to be interventionist, some more than others. The private sector resents that interventionism yet, paradoxically, holds government responsible for inadequate national economic performance. As a result, the nature of public/private relations in Canada is never clear and oscillates between extremes. But the partnership that characterizes public sector/private sector relations in other countries (such as Japan and others) is usually absent in Canada, but when present, is not particularly successful.

The third adversary system places labour in direct opposition to management. In the face of turbulence and rapid economic change, labour tries to protect itself by being vigilant. Management, in turn, will naturally tend to place competitiveness and profits high on the priority list. As a result, industrial relations are adversarial and Canada has earned the dubious distinction of competing with Italy for top honours in days lost to strikes for most of the decade of the seventies.

The fourth major adversary system opposes small Canadian firms against each other. True enough, competition is the essence of the market system but its proper place is the subject of new thinking in strategic theory. Should Canadians destroy each other and then let home markets be taken over by giant multinationals? Or should they, instead, form alliances like the Japanese and French firms do to compete in the international marketplace?

The answers are not simple. They require subtle analysis, and blanket statements are inappropriate. However, what appears to be a fact is that, because of distance, because of regionalism, because of the gravitational attraction of the United States, the system of governance in Canada has strayed away from consensus into an institutionalized conflict system, with multiple interfaces. There is evidence to show that adversarial relations have kept Canadian performance well below potential and have imprisoned the country in a mode of mediocrity, which is all the more distressing in that it is eminently avoidable.

Let us now examine each of the systems in turn and identify alternatives to the adversarial mode.

Chapter 5

RETHINKING CONFEDERATION AFTER MEECH

Canada and the United States:
A Tale of Two Federations.

Canada was initially conceived as "British North America". The name was apt. The principal binding link between its elements was indeed the British Crown. The design of Confederation in 1867 followed the pattern of 'divide and rule' which was to become a British legacy to ex-colonies.

In Canada's case, power was apportioned between the federal and provincial governments and the Parliament at Westminster reserved for itself the ultimate prerogative of arbitration of disputes. However, many areas of jurisdiction were left ambiguous and open to interpretation. Therefore, as Canadian society became more complex, these 'residual powers' became the object of strong competition between the levels of government. This was the historical root of the federal/provincial adversary system of today.

From its genesis, in 1867, through its contemporary modifications, (patriation in 1981 and the Meech Lake Accord signed in preliminary form by the eleven first ministers in 1987), the Canadian Confederation evolved along a path quite opposite to that of its southern neighbour the United States. In the United States, much more was defined than was left out in the original constitution, so that the areas of ambivalence were limited. In addition, the American political system has evolved in the direction of a centralized federation with the president of the United States emerging as the undisputed chief executive. The Americans realized very early that only a strong central government would keep the Union together.

In addition, as far as federal/state responsibilities are concerned, the exercise of power over the years has clearly established the supremacy of the federal authority. The Americans even fought a civil war on that point. The southern states, interested in maintaining their distinctness (in that case, the right legally to own slaves), argued for a confederal or looser union. The northern states resisted that notion. The ensuing civil war settled the point in blood, with the centralist federalists defeating the decentralizing confederalists. As a result, the United States evolved into the strong federation it is now, headed by a chief executive officer possessing legal powers which, in some other countries, would be considered dictatorial. The office of president of the United States is truly the most powerful elected job in the world.

The centralizing bias in the United States was reinforced in the cultural field by the alternatively celebrated and maligned American 'melting pot'. Realizing that a country of immigrants like the United States could only become great by building a culture of its own, the Americans created a 'melting pot' whose primary objective was the psychological rejection of the old country by the newly-arrived immigrants. The latter had the option of adopting a new name and, with it, new values. These values, based on the 'not-Europe' or 'not-old country' theme, were to be constructed on the foundations of American political theory - that is on the 'pursuit of happiness, liberty and (implicitly), private property and wealth'. The American 'melting pot' has created an

identifiable American culture. It may be considered good
or bad depending on one's point of view, but no one can
claim that it does not exist.

Canada's union, on the other hand, followed a very
different course. In the first place, federal/provincial
relations were set on an alternating mode of spurts of
centralization/decentralization. The natural centrifugal
trend was counterbalanced by initiatives such as the late
nineteenth century National Policy and more contemporary
twentieth century forms of centralism. Historians still
argue about what was the net effect of all this. Some argue
that the federal government ended up gaining power over
the provincial governments. This is a difficult point to
prove, especially in a comparative world-context where the
Canadian federation probably ranks as one of the most
decentralized nations on earth.

In Canada's Constitution, the provinces are
sovereign in certain areas of jurisdiction. There is no clear
hierarchy between levels of government. Federal Cabinet
ministers must treat provincial ministers as their
counterparts, not as their subordinates. Even the
terminology supports this idea. In French, all eleven
government leaders are 'prime ministers', ten provincial
and one federal. In English, a distinction is made between
provincial 'premiers' and the 'prime minister of Canada' but
even this distinction is glossed-over when we stage our
periodic 'First Ministers Conferences' where there is a
general presumption of equality. The head of the federal
government acts as convenor or chairman, but is not
supposed to 'pull rank' over the others. There are many
areas of overlapping jurisdiction: the 1867 Founding
Fathers could not possibly have conceived of everything
that was going to happen in the twentieth century and

assign to it a federal or provincial status. As a result, in many realms of public policy not one but eleven voices speak for Canada. With the addition of the Territories the eleven voices have become thirteen.

A second important difference between the two federations is that in Canada the prime minister, although quite powerful, is much less so than his American counterpart. In the first place he is not the head of state - a position which is held by the Governor-General; the President of the United States, on the other hand, is subordinate to no one and is, himself, the head of state. In the second place, a Canadian prime minister occupies that post courtesy of a majority of his party in the House of Commons. There is no separation of powers here. We imported the full British parliamentary tradition on that point. Consequently, the Canadian prime minister's mandate does not come directly from the people, but only indirectly, since he must first be chosen to lead his party and then must win a majority in the House of Commons. In addition, in Canada the provincial premiers wield much greater power than U.S. governors. They can, in effect, successfully oppose the initiatives of the federal prime minister, either collectively or singly, if they come from a powerful province like Ontario or Quebec. This fact was well illustrated, in 1988, when the United States required provincial endorsement of the Free Trade Accord, knowing full well that without that endorsement the Accord would be difficult to enforce. No demand has been heard from the Canadian government for approval by the individual states of the United States, because of the realization that they are much less powerful than Canadian provinces.

A third major difference between the two federations is that the U.S. central government reflects not only the national purpose but also the interests of the individual states in the U.S. Senate; *in the Canadian situation, the provinces are legally absent from the federal scene.*

Canada's Parliament is a more or less faithful replica of Westminster, both visually and conceptually. Some observers now feel that this was a mistake. Westminster, the mother of parliaments, was conceived to implement democracy in a small island nation with a unitary government. The Canadian Senate draws its inspiration from the British House of Lords - a non-elected gathering of senior dignitaries who have been rewarded for past services to the nation. Britain rewards distinguished national service with a peerage, Canada with a seat in the Senate. The Senate represents no particular body. It could have been a House of the Provinces, similar to its U.S. counterpart where two senators represent each state of the union independent of size. The required U.S. Senate approval, not only of legislation but also of senior government appointments, allows the states to be an integral part of the U.S. federal government.

In Canada, on the contrary, the provinces are not legally part of the federal government. This has resulted (and could only have resulted) in one thing: *the exacerbation of the federal/provincial adversary system, since there is no perceived goal congruence between the provincial purpose and the national purpose.* Consequently, federal/provincial conferences tend to degenerate into political auctions where opposing interests confront each other and where the noisiest and squeakiest wheels get the most attention. The federal government then has to give and take in classical negotiating mode. 'Brownie points' are obtained by provincial premiers if they come home laden with 'goodies' from what is viewed as a fixed-size basket. In all, the design of the system clearly favours the adversarial mode.

Issues on the Confederation Agenda

As the nineties are upon us, the question of the adequacy of the design of Canada's confederation will probably revolve around at least four major issues. These are: (a) the Quebec/Canada relationship in all its complexity; (b) the federal/provincial relationship; (c) the provincial/provincial relationship and (d) the possible strengthening of the municipal level of government and its consequences. Each of these major issues must be viewed in the light of the growing continentalization of the Canadian economy, spearheaded by the Free Trade Accord but obviously going much beyond it, as was shown in earlier chapters.

The Quebec/Canada Issue

At the heart of the Canadian dilemma is the Quebec/Canada issue. Given the realities of the continental economy, we must actually consider a triangular relationship, since many of the questions that arise in the Canada-United States problem set have counterparts in the Quebec/Canada arena. What Canada seeks at the North American level is, in effect, what the Parti Québécois wanted from Canada: a sovereignty-association - political sovereignty and economic association.

Francophone Quebec's view of Canada has historically been characterized by three features: (a) the desire to preserve its distinct character, (b) the desire to keep Canada alive and (c) a perception of English Canada as a homogeneous whole. The preservation of Quebec's

distinctiveness has been a perennial feature of Quebec
politics since the Seven Years War and the Battle of the
Plains of Abraham. Quebec's motto "Je me souviens" is
indicative of this mood. What does Quebec remember
exactly?: probably its status as a separate society with its
own values, mores, language and tradition and, therefore,
its own agenda for change.

This perception may vary in intensity between
provincial Liberals, Conservatives, Péquistes and hard-core
Separatists. But we are talking about shades of gray, not
major differences in colour. Thus the 'red' provincial
Liberals tend to be on some issues as nationalist as their
Péquiste colleagues, if not more so. Similarly the 'blue'
Péquistes will not hesitate to ally themselves temporarily
with a Conservative 'blue' government in Ottawa to pursue
Quebec's interests.

The preservation of the distinct character of this
province-nation is an unwritten axiom of Quebec's policies
with respect to Ottawa, endorsed by Duplessis, Lesage
(who introduced the idea of the 'state' of Quebec), Daniel
Johnson (Egalité ou Indépendance), Bourassa (the
insistence on maintaining a Quebec veto in constitutional
matters), René Lévesque (sovereignty-association) and
again Bourassa (Meech Lake Accord).

Front and centre in Quebec's perception of itself in
Canada is the primacy of the language issue. Except for a
few Québécois assimilated into the English majority in
Canada, all others of French descent or expression believe
in the paramount necessity of defending the French
language. Challenge that perceived necessity and trouble
ensues. Promise anything different than the supremacy of
French in an electoral campaign and, at delivery time, be
prepared for major conflict. Hence the wise policy is

"keep French dominant, keep language policy strict and vigilant". In Quebec, to take an opposing view is to court electoral disaster whether one is 'red', 'blue' or 'green'.

The second part of Quebec's perception is a genuine interest in maintaining a strong Canada. Certainly all but the most radical indépendantistes would be dismayed at the thought of the collapse of English Canada and its absorption by the United States. This stake in English Canada's continued health is rooted in two ideas.

First, there is a family affinity for some of the things English Canada stands for. The Québécois were after all the original *Canadiens,* and they share with today's English 'Canadians' a certain grounding in the 'not-America' theme.

The second is more pragmatic. If English Canada were to join the United States, Quebec would find itself in a very difficult geopolitical position: six million Québécois surrounded by 270 million English-speaking Americans. To prevent that disturbing scenario from occurring, English Canada must remain independent from the United States. The solution: *Un Québec indépendant dans un Canada fort,* as a Quebec popular singer once put it or "an independent Quebec in a strong Canada" - an admirably well-expressed statement of Quebec's candid ambivalence towards Canada.

This ambivalence is usually expressed in voting patterns where, from 1976 to 1984, the same Quebec voters would send a strong centralist Trudeau government to Ottawa and an equally strong anti-centralist government to Québec City. *Vote red for Ottawa and blue for Québec City or vice-versa, but avoid if possible voting red or blue in both places.* Quebec's interests are best served by maintaining different focuses and different agendas.

Quebec's ambivalence towards Canada is also expressed within political parties. For instance, within the ranks of Quebec 'reds' there are three liberal parties: the PLQ or Provincial Liberal Party, the PLC or Federal Liberal Party and the PLC(Q) or Quebec wing of the Federal Liberal Party. Relationships between the PLC and the PLQ have always been ambivalent. Officially the two parties have nothing in common but the coincidence of the name. Ideologically, the Quebec Liberal Party, in 1987-1988, under Premier Bourassa was more to the right than its federal counterpart. It favoured many more privatizations and state-minimization initiatives than the national party. In addition, there was direct opposition as far as the Free Trade Accord was concerned. The provincial Liberals were enthusiastic supporters of free trade with the United States while the federal Liberals, under John Turner, were diametrically opposed. Yet, quite often, the same militants belonged to both parties. How did they resolve that issue? With their provincial hats they clamoured for free trade, while in federal party conventions they decried its effects on Canadian sovereignty.

As for the party leadership, Premier Bourassa made it quite clear, in 1988, that he intended to remain neutral on the federal scene. In contrast, other provincial Liberal, Conservative or NDP Parties were much closer to their national counterparts than were the corresponding parties in Quebec. It would have been rather odd for a Liberal premier of Ontario not to endorse the federal Liberals or for NDP premiers to proclaim their neutrality with respect to Ed Broadbent's party.

An additional expression of Quebec's distinctiveness is the duality within the federal parties. The

PLC(Q) is in many senses an independent party with its own agenda and its own policy committees loosely federated to the national party. Ontario has similar structures but the autonomy of the Quebec wing is, in practice, greater than that of other provinces.

The third element in Quebec's perception of Canada is its view of English Canada as a strong, unified entity speaking with one voice. Evidence suggests, on the other hand, that 'English Canada' is a Quebec invention and has no reality, save possibly with respect to Quebec itself. The differences between the agendas of Ontario, the Prairies, British Columbia, the Maritimes and Newfoundland are enormous. Quebec erroneously believes that English Canada equals Ontario and that if a modus vivendi were to be arrived at with that province, all would be 'fine and dandy'. Ontario is Quebec's ultimate reference point. The other provinces are often psychologically perceived as sub-sets of Ontario.

This fallacy has important consequences. It means that Quebec believes it can pursue its policy of cultivating its distinctiveness without upsetting the delicate balance within so-called English Canada. Yet, there is reason to believe that Canada without Quebec would not be a viable proposition. The Maritimes, cut off from the rest of the country, would quite naturally look south to the United States. So would Alberta, for different reasons.

As a former senior official of PEI once mentioned, "Canada is like a boring party, where the guests are too polite to leave. However, when the first guest makes a move to go, the others each claim other engagements and make a quick exit."

If Quebec were to leave Confederation, are there enough binding links between the other provinces to keep the Club alive? Let us now look at the question from the vantage point of the rest of Canada.

The Federal/Provincial Relationship

Is Canada a 'crazy-glue' nation which will come apart at the seams? How strong is the national relationship? As was argued earlier, continentalist forces are very strong in the country and the attempt to make Vancouver Island and Newfoundland part of the same economic unit called Canada is a major undertaking. Historically, what has kept the provinces together is, first and foremost, fear of the United States and second, fear of Quebec separation.

But in order to accommodate Quebec, the federal/provincial relationship had to evolve in the direction of decentralization, with unanticipated consequences. Beyond a certain point, concessions to Quebec could not be granted without similar concessions being accorded to the other provinces. Thus the process of devolution of power accelerated.

The structure of the Canadian economy, with no public sector intervention, but coupled with legal and economic barriers at the 49th parallel, strongly favour Central Canada. People, capital, technology and resources would tend to rush to the centre. In fact, in spite of regional equalization policies and strong public sector intervention, factors of production in Canada have, indeed, tended to flock to Ontario.

The unemployment rate was always negligible in Ontario while it remained quite high in the peripheral provinces. Beyond the industrial heartland (the Quebec-Windsor Corridor) where 50 percent of all Canadians live, the rest of the country can be described as being long stretches of unoccupied empty land interspersed with a few urban concentrations here and there. Some of these urban concentrations receive public sector support. Without such support they would either not exist or be much smaller. Thus, it can be accurately stated that a number of urban units outside the Corridor thrive only because of 'artificial respiration'. Without such artificial respiration, provided by federal transfers, what would happen?

Before free trade the answer was obvious. Many factors of production would move to Ontario and Quebec. With free trade the answer is less obvious. Instead of moving to Ontario and Quebec, people and capital may move south and west to the Sunbelt, especially if we end-up having a common market with the United States. The comparative advantages of the Snowbelt in which we live, are much less obvious. The Sunbelt is, on the other hand, increasingly attractive. There are smaller energy costs, a higher quality of life and a number of opportunities that at present do not exist here.

One part of Canada whose future is particularly uncertain, because of the twin effects of free trade and Meech Lake, is the Maritimes region. As was noted earlier, it is unlikely in the event of an independent Quebec that these provinces would remain indefinitely within Canada. Not particularly resource-rich with the exception of fish products and oil, they have tended to export people and ideas to Central Canada. This process has been slowed, somewhat, by federal policies destined to create development poles in that part of the country. If these policies are reduced or eliminated because of the evolution of Confederation, and if a common market with the United States becomes a reality, it is likely that a net outflow of people will occur - no longer towards Ontario but now towards New England and points south.

The Provincial/Provincial Relationship

The relationships among provincial governments is another issue in the design of an optimum federation for Canada. In the present system, the provinces have only indirect relationships with each other, since the major interface occurs within First Ministers Conferences. However, a number of exceptions must be noted.

First, regional groupings of provinces have emerged. The spatial configuration of Canada encourages a commonality of interests among say, the Prairie provinces on the one hand, and the Maritime and Atlantic provinces on the other. The Council of Maritime Premiers, for instance, is an example of such a grouping. In practice, these groupings tend to be informal and have only limited effectiveness, although the potential for extensive collaboration is there. On the whole, however, inter-provincial relations in Canada, outside the federal/provincial mould, have been characterized by adversarial initiatives and/or duplication or cancellation of efforts.

The adversarial mode stems from the fact that each province perceives the national 'pie' as fixed in size. The maximization of each province's share of that 'pie' is, therefore, a priority. This means outbidding other provinces for federal contracts, for the location of industrial parks, space agencies and military projects. Whichever province can bring to the table more political clout will win in the end.

Duplication of effort is a second major feature of inter-provincial relations. Once provincial governments recognized the importance of high technology, every province wanted its own 'Silicon Valley'. This has led to immense duplication of effort on the national scale, where high technology centres with almost identical mandates sprouted throughout the land. There has been very little effort to co-ordinate activities and arrive at some form of division of labour. This is becoming true in all areas of high technology, from space research to biotechnology and robotics. Everyone wants the same things.

Thirdly and perhaps more importantly, inter-provincial rivalry has taken the form of non-tariff barriers which greatly reduce free trade within Canada, let alone between Canada and the United States. The procurement policies of each provincial government tend to favour locals over out-of-province suppliers. Therefore, if a Quebec firm wished to obtain Ontario contracts or vice-versa it should ultimately establish branch plants in the client market.

Inter-provincial trade barriers also take the form of different tax systems, explicit and implicit subsidies and other general distortions of trade. In the end, if provincial governments were to decide to go full blast into major 'industrial strategies' we could run the risk of having ten competing strategies vying for a greater share of the national 'pie', come what may, with, as a probable result, a smaller overall 'pie'.

The Adversarial Mode at the Municipal Level

The third, and sometimes forgotten, level of government is the municipal. Although clearly subordinate to the other two, the municipal level is, nevertheless, the locus of considerable public-sector activity. The major cities of Canada are each developing their own agendas and there is a clear temptation for some of them to move into a 'city-state' frame of mind. This is true, in particular, for Montreal, Toronto, Vancouver and Halifax, each in its own way the focus of great economic activity and a development pole in its region.

The relationship between major cities in Canada is, like other key relationships within the Canadian system, adversarial. A number of traditional rivalries persist and are enhanced. There is the perennial rivalry between Montreal and Toronto for economic dominance. The current supremacy of Toronto is not necessarily permanent. As the former metropolis of Canada, Montreal seeks to enhance its international role and attract head-offices of major corporations, international organizations and federal government agencies. The impact of free trade may conceivably reduce the relative importance of Toronto and increase that of Montreal whose 'product differentiation' on the North American scene is much greater than Toronto's.

Added to the Montreal/Toronto duel is Ottawa-Hull's competition with both. The area receives major support from the activities of the federal government. The development of high technology firms in the Kanata Valley is directly attributable to the presence of that government and its procurement and R&D policies. The three cities, Toronto, Ottawa and Montreal constitute what has sometimes been called the 'TOM Triangle'. This urban network could conceivably develop specialization of functions and diversify in harmony rather than in opposition.

For example, there are at least two other urban trios abroad which have in fact divided the labour among the member cities. In Switzerland, Berne is the national capital and the administrative centre, Zurich the uncontested financial centre and Geneva the unchallenged seat of many international agencies. In a similar vein, in Brazil, Brasilia is the national capital, Sao Paolo the principal financial and economic centre and Rio de Janeiro, the capital of the arts, of glamour, of culture and international influence. Canada's Rio would be Montreal, Sao Paolo resembles Toronto and Brasilia is obviously the counterpart of Ottawa-Hull.

If TOM were organized as a strong urban network, based on rapid inter-city transit and complementary support functions, then it could develop into a world-class megalopolis with immense advantages. If, on the other hand, the adversarial mode were to continue to dominate, mutual neutralization would result and there would be less than world-class competitiveness for each and every one of these three cities. The separate advantages of these three snow-bound cities in a North American economic union are less compelling than the integrated power of all three in combination. A world-class TOM could definitely be a 'trump card' for Canada. But it would require seeking complementarities rather than fighting to the end over every crumb.

The competitive-adversarial mode between municipalities is also very present in the Maritimes where Halifax is seen as the 'bad guy' by all the other cities. Indeed, Moncton, Fredericton, St. John, Amherst and Charlottetown measure their success and failure in life by comparison with Halifax. The drive to cut Halifax down to size and to prevent that regional metropolis from absorbing the best resources of its hinterland is behind many development initiatives of the rival cities.

Even on a smaller scale, throughout the country, the competition between municipalities is very strong. One possible direction for the future is that with the devolution of power from the central to the provincial governments, municipalities will, in turn, demand greater autonomy. Today, the adversarial mode in Canadian politics allows for a quasi-diplomatic representation of Canadian provinces abroad. Thus 'Ontario Houses', 'British Columbia Houses' and 'Maisons du Québec', located in major cities around the globe, attempt to attract investment, technology, trade and people to their respective provinces. Sometimes, these missions abroad compete directly with the Canadian embassies in the same host country.

This practice is, to some extent, a peculiarity of Canada. Few other countries go that far. There is, for instance, no 'House of Prussia' or 'House of Bavaria' in the major cities of the world. Nor are there New York State and California Houses systematically competing against each other in the leading capitals of Europe. Yet, both West Germany and the United States are federal countries and could, if they had a system similar to ours, promote that kind of para-diplomatic representation. Most if not all of American foreign policy is mediated by the U.S. State Department and American Embassies abroad, not by individual state governments.

What is also interesting to note is that the para-diplomatic representation of provinces is now being advocated for cities.

An institute has recently been formed in Montreal to examine the international role of cities. One of its recommendations is that major cities like Montreal, Toronto and Vancouver should compete head-on in the international marketplace. Alongside the Canadian Embassy in Paris and the High Commission in London there would then be not only a number of Houses representing provincial interests but, in addition, para-diplomatic missions to represent competing cities. If that were to happen, then the internal adversarial mode would have reached its international apex.

The Meech Lake Dilemma

The Meech Lake Accord, signed in preliminary form in the spring of 1987 by the eleven First Ministers, is supposed to set the stage for a renewed Confederation. It is meant to achieve a balance between the need for national unity and the legitimate regional, ethnic and provincial differences that exist in this country. As in the case of the Free Trade Agreement, the Accord is couched in advanced 'legalese' which has confounded so far even the constitutional experts. At the time of writing (late 1989), the fate of the Meech Lake Accord was uncertain. Would it be passed by all the provinces by the deadline? One way or the other, whether the Accord becomes the law of the land or not, it will have marked the Canadian confederation. Let us now speculate on each of the two possible outcomes.

The Meech Lake Accord is similar to the Free Trade Agreement in at least three respects. First, both Accords are immensely complex. In the case of free trade, full mastery of the implications of the agreement requires advanced knowledge of international economics, international law and comparative public policies. In the case of the Meech Lake Accord, a thorough grounding in constitutional law, jurisprudence and inter-governmental relations is a pre-condition for understanding its intricacies. Since very few Canadians possess these combinations of skills, the ultimate meaning of each of the two accords will be left to the courts - Canadian courts for Meech Lake, American and international courts for free trade.

No definitive statements, therefore, can be made at this time by anyone. As eminent experts disagree, laymen should stay clear of the technical debate. Former Prime Minister Pierre Trudeau believes Meech Lake to be calamitous for Canada while other members of his adminstration believe it to be essential. If it ever comes to that, the Supreme Court of Canada will be called upon to judge some of the meanings of the accord and, even then, it is unclear whether all provinces would necessarily accept the interpretation.

The second aspect of the Meech Lake Accord, which makes it a close cousin of the Free Trade Agreement, is that both tend to be more 'declaratory' than 'constitutive'. A 'declaratory' statement in law recognizes a fact or a quality that is deemed to exist already. A 'constitutive' statement creates a new situation. In the case of free trade, much of the liberalization of commerce between the United States and Canada had already taken place before January 1989. The Free Trade Agreement did not objectively change that much. By the same token, it may be strictly true that in recognizing Quebec as a distinct society, the Meech Lake Accord does not go beyond accepted Canadian practice in the last half-century. From a purely legalistic point of view, it may be that Meech Lake does not create fundamentally new powers for the provinces.

But the third aspect that both Accords have in common is, by far, the most significant. We are talking about *psychological effects.* As was shown in Chapter 2, many businessmen and the general public mistakenly believed that trade between the United States and Canada was not 'free' prior to January 1989 and that it has become 'free' since. The myth of the massive tariff wall has prompted many to vote for free trade under mistaken assumptions. The psychological effects on both sides of the border, and in Europe and Asia, will slowly unfold over the years and they are, as we have seen, both positive and

negative. People are viewing Canada in a new light. Some
see it as a *back door to* the United States and, therefore,
attractive.   Others see it as a *back yard of* the United
States and not so attractive. Impressions predominate, not
the real thing.

In the case of Meech Lake, the psychological
effects will also engender a number of policy thrusts,
which may or may not be fully substantiated by the legal
aspects of the agreement itself. What are these thrusts?

First, the Meech Lake Agreement transfers some
power from the executive to the judiciary branch of
government. The Supreme Court of Canada will be asked
to rule on what were hitherto political questions. Every
major case may take years and, for this reason, issues will
remain unsettled for long periods of time.

Second, there is a tendency to transfer spending
power, over the long run, from the federal to the provincial
governments. In 1986, the federal government controlled
about 45 percent of public sector spending. The rest was
controlled by the provincial and municipal governments
and various para-public corporations. Of the 45 percent
that was federally controlled, about 15 percent went to
federal-provincial transfers and was actually spent by the
provinces. What will happen in the future?

The new spirit of a decentralized confederation
emphasizing distinctiveness, spearheaded by Meech Lake
but also reinforced by the 'notwithstanding clause' in the
Charter of Rights, leads to more devolution of power from
the central to other levels of government. One outcome
could be that the federal government, in the year 2,000,
will control less than 20 percent of public sector spending
in Canada. In other words, it will have become a bit player
on the national scene, no longer strong enough to regulate

the economy. Counter-cyclical fiscal policies will now
have to be arrived-at by consensus, since the federal
government alone will no longer have the power to
implement them.   One can visualize First Ministers
Conferences, early in the twenty-first century, trying to
achieve common policies - with Ontario wanting to cool
the economy down and the weaker provinces wanting to
stimulate it. The federal government would not be able to
resolve the issue. Hence, contradictory policies could coexist, with unpredictable consequences.

A third potential effect of Meech is the ambiguity
of the 'distinctiveness' clause itself and the possibility that
it will eventually be claimed by many other groups. The
first such group could be the native peoples. Their claim to
distinctiveness is certainly older than anyone else's and
probably even more legitimate. Not to recognize their
rights in the future will be to open the door to potential
trouble. The radicalization of the native peoples is a clear
possibility and if they begin to claim sovereignty-
association, it should not come as a surprise.

Beyond the native people, the country is large and
diverse enough to support other claims of distinctiveness.
For instance, the premier of Alberta claimed, in June 1988,
that Alberta, too, was a distinct society and if it chose not
to translate legislation into French it was well within its
rights. Ultimately, the danger is that the country will
become a collection of distinct groupings whose *common*
purpose will become more and more obscure.

On the other side of the ledger are the clearly
positive aspects of the Meech Lake Accord. First and
foremost, the spirit of Meech has brought about a period of
federal government/Quebec government co-operation
which was unheard of before. It has also led to a greater

understanding between provinces who have recognized their individual rights to go their separate ways. Thus, in the spring of 1988, Premier Bourassa preferred to support the Manitoba government decisions against the use of French in that province rather than back the Francophones there.

The optimistic view of Meech is that once Canada's diversity is not only recognized, but enshrined in the Constitution, a climate of long-term co-operation between provinces and between the federal and provincial governments will prevail. What had not been achieved legally would then be arrived at informally - through consultation and consensus. Time will tell whether this particular view will be proved correct.

Another positive aspect of Meech is that it does bring Quebec back into Confederation. There are those who claim that if the Meech Lake Accord were to fail, Quebec would be so resentful that it would become very nationalist once again. Others claim, on the contrary, that Meech is just the first step towards a new sovereignty-association, clearly rejected by the voters in the 1981 referendum but resurfacing in a new form in the Meech Lake Accord.

Meech Lake is, in some senses, yet another of the compromises for which Canada is so famous. It distances itself from the Trudeau vision of a highly centralized federation by transferring power away from the federal government and decentralizing the decision-making process. It does not go as far as the Parti Québécois wanted, since it refuses to grant sovereignty to Quebec and instead recognizes its distinct character, whatever that will be interpreted to mean by the courts. It is not quite in the middle of the two options, since it tilts closer to the péquiste option than it does to the Trudeau vision. But, for all intents and purposes, it is still a black box, an ink-blot, an ambiguous document to be made explicit by the passage of time.

In many senses, it is quite conservative as it affirms a number of aspects of Canada which are already obvious, such as Quebec's distinctiveness. But it also opens up a number of new avenues by solidifying some elements of the adversarial mode, while at the same time providing a climate for informal concentration of effort and co-ordination of purpose. Judgement on it must be reserved until the other elements of the puzzle are in: the state/society issue, the labour/management interface and the nature of our private sector economy - elements to which we now turn.

Chapter 6

RETHINKING THE STATE :
SHOULD THE GORGING LEVIATHAN
BECOME ANOREXIC ? *

(* This chapter was published in earlier form in the
Canadian Journal of Administrative Studies , December
1987 and won a prize from the Max Bell Foundation for
Business/Government Relations in Canada).

The public sector/private sector interface is a major
issue in contemporary Canada and one that is germane to
the future of Confederation. The uncontrolled growth of
government, over the past fifteen years, in most of the
OECD countries has revived a debate that used to be
purely ideological: what is the proper role of the state in a
modern economy? The traditional answers used to
gravitate along a conventional 'left-right' axis and were
based on *a priori* notions of how society should function.

Now, however, the question has transcended
ideology and has spilled over to become a management
question: given increasing social complexity, how should
government relate to the private sector? As *referee* to
ensure the proper functioning of sovereign markets? As
antidote to social injustice? As direct *entrepreneur?* As
captain of the national competitive team pursuing world
markets, as *catalyst for change* - or merely as cleaner of
the streets, a function which itself is being increasingly
privatized.

The phenomenal expansion of government
activities in the recent past has led to intractable deficits
and debt problems, giving this question an urgency that it
is likely to retain to the end of this century. Yet it appears

that the contemporary response to this challenge deepens the problem rather than resolves it. Ideological stances aside, no satisfactory model exists to describe optimum state participation in our modern economy. The principal attempts of the last two decades to deal with the problem of the proper role of government have been the 'maximum state' experiment of the seventies and its 'minimum state' negation which is currently fashionable. The 'maximum state' approach has led to what the British periodical, *The Economist* , has aptly called a "Gorging Leviathan" with an insatiable appetite and disruptive behaviour. Its putative successor, the 'minimum state' model, attempts to starve Leviathan into submission. In the process, however, it is in danger of trapping governments into a disease similar to *anorexia nervosa* - lean and compulsive austerity, loss of creative energy, the shedding of muscle in addition to fat, the whole based on the almost religious belief that the state, by definition, can do no right and is a congenital bungler.

There is evidence that neither public sector gorging nor a starvation diet are appropriate responses to the challenges of the contemporary world, and that we must seek intermediate models. An outline of some such models, based on the idea of an *organic* partnership between the public and private sectors, will be presented at the end of this chapter, although a full exposition of what is entailed would require the broader context of a separate book.

The Gorging Leviathan: The Rise and Fall of the Maximum State.

There is an interesting asymmetry between the 'maximum' and 'minimum' state theses. There have been comparatively few theoretical expositions of why we should have a maximum state, *yet its most hostile opponents have contributed to its rise.*

At the same time, the literature abounds with treatises on why a minimum state is desirable, but for all practical purposes *it has yet to have been tried anywhere.* The Reagan experiment in the United States, the most touted contemporary attempt at state-minimization, has resulted in a much greater public deficit than before it was attempted: a deficit legitimated by military expenditures. The Thatcher experiment in Britain has been far from conclusive, since deficit reduction has been achieved by selling-off public capital in the form of the privatization of state-owned companies. Here in Canada, both the federal Conservatives and the Quebec Liberals rose to power on minimum state platforms, in 1984 and 1985 respectively. Both, in their first terms of office, have retreated in the face of political pressure and ended-up only marginally modifying previous policies.

Politicians write about minimum government and consistently practice maximum government. Why is this? Is it because they are inherently dishonest? Is it attributable to the frailty of human nature? Or has the complexity of today's problems rendered our *a priori* theories inoperable? To answer this question let us first look at the record of growth in government activities over the past fifteen years, in order to identify its nature and causes.

The Expansion of Government 1960 - 1982.

In 1960, in only two OECD countries did government expenditures amount to more than one-third of gross domestic product (GDP). Between 1960 and 1982, the average size of government expenditure rose 20 percentage points in relation to nominal GDP. The average annual increase was 2.75 percent and, in 1982, all OECD countries, *of whatever political persuasion,* had levels of government expenditures above one-third of GDP - with the average being 47 percent versus 27 percent in 1960. By 1984, state spending had levelled to about 45 percent of GDP, with a minimum of 33 percent in Switzerland versus a maximum of 64 percent in Sweden.

At that time, transfer payments were the largest economic category, accounting for over half of total public spending. In contrast, government investment declined both in relation to GDP and to total spending by government. The structure of government expenditure shifted away from traditional collective goods (defence, administration and social services) towards welfare state expenditures (education, health and income supplements) that provide individual rather than collective benefits. One cause of increased health spending has been the rise in average life expectancy by four years.

In 1960, public final consumption expenditure was 15.5 percent of total expenditure, while in 1982, it rose to 23 percent. As direct employer of labour, government increased from 11 percent in 1960 to 18 percent in 1982. In 1960, households received 20 percent of their income from government and returned 15 percent in the form of taxes. In 1982, government payments to households accounted for 30 percent of their income and 24 percent was returned in the form of income taxes and social security contributions.

In order to finance its growth, government resorted to taxing the sources of income, in addition to its uses and to widescale borrowing. In 1960, government borrowing absorbed 14 percent of gross domestic savings, while in

1982, this ratio went up to 22 percent. Debt interest, for example, had risen to 7 percent of public spending in 1975, and reached 14 percent of public spending in the United States in 1986.

The growth of government expenditure had very different effects in the sixties than in the seventies. The sixties was a period of strong expansion of the world economy. The growth of the public sector, in this context, seemed relatively harmless and appeared necessary to maintain social consensus. The state adopted the role of Great Equalizer (appropriately reflected in the Kennedy-Johnson "Great Society" and Trudeau's "Just Society" programmes).

In the seventies, on the other hand, different conditions emerged. First, there was an unparalleled boom in food and commodity prices; this left producing nations living the easy life of the *rentier* on the one hand and consumer nations hard-pressed on the other. This situation was, of course, symbolized by the rise in energy prices that accompanied the two oil shocks of 1973 and 1979. It was also reflected in a general inflation of raw materials prices.

Second, there was a general decline in economic performance, as a result of the oil shocks, which manifested itself in 'stagflation' - economic stagnation accompanied by high inflation.

Third, in order to meet the challenges of the first two, government assumed the roles of counter-cyclical balancer and social services provider. Safety-net creation and building cushions against external shocks became standard government functions. These functions were incorporated into a general 'welfare state' ideology, itself reflecting a new political consensus. The power of labour unions and the desire to obtain larger shares of a shrinking 'pie' moved the political spectrum in the Western world clearly to left of centre. Social democracy prevailed and to finance the growing responsibilities of the state, governments increased direct and indirect taxes, bloated their civil services and borrowed extensively. The 'maximum state' was born less out of pure ideology than out of a force of circumstances and the political reality.

The Limits to State Expansion.

By the beginning of the eighties, the public sector moved from being the solution to becoming the main problem. The oil shock, of 1979, triggered a severe recession two years later and the rising burden of world debt and fiscal deficits led to fundamental questioning of the wisdom of continued, unbridled expansion of state activities. Once again, independent of ideology, governments of different political persuasions decided to go on a 'reducing diet'. The need for this reduction came from at least three sources.

The first danger signal came from the nature of government spending, which became increasingly inefficient and wasteful. The trend was towards the bureaucratization of the economy, with private sector entrepreneurs being transformed into public sector functionaries - only interested in collecting their salaries and relying on their unions to obtain for them the maximum possible share of the nation's wealth. This led to fears of the dreaded 'British disease': excessive state intervention, subsidies and overall inefficiency crowding-out productive activity. Throwing dollars at a problem with taxpayers' money did not seem to resolve anything.

The second danger signal came from the limits of taxation. The ability of the private sector to absorb further tax increases was reaching its ceiling. The burden of the income tax reached intolerable proportions and generally became a disincentive to productivity and work.

In 1979, maximum marginal income tax rates were 55 percent in Canada, 56 percent in West Germany, 70 percent in Japan, and 90 percent in Sweden. By 1984, a family of four, with a $45,000 income, would pay a marginal rate of 34 percent in Switzerland, 45 percent in France, 48 percent in West Germany, 53 percent in Italy, 60 percent in Britain, 64 percent in Denmark and Austria, and 90 percent in Sweden. At these rates, there was little incentive to work any harder.

The third signal was the danger associated with *borrowing*. Uncontrolled public borrowing created distortions in financial markets, a crowding-out effect on private borrowing and very high interest rates. These, in turn, fuelled inflation and worsened an international debt crisis, where the servicing of public debts absorbed an increasing proportion of public funds.

The three sets of danger signals combined with a reversal of the direction of oil prices and a disinflationary trend to strengthen a new movement. In full fashion for most of the eighties, the new movement was advocacy of the 'minimum state'.

The Case For and Against the Minimum State

The case for the 'minimum state' is based on the virtues of competitive markets and the unworkability of command economies. The first and most persuasive advocate of the minimum state, Adam Smith, laid the foundation of classical capitalist economics. In his celebrated *Inquiry into the Nature and Causes of the Wealth of Nations*, he showed how competitive markets create specialization within a country and internationally.

This division of labour is both efficient and wealth-producing - as economists, over the last two hundred years, have confirmed both logically and mathematically. Indeed, most post-Smithian classical economics - extolling the efficiency of free markets in wealth production - is but a lengthy footnote to the original Smithian recommendations of *laisser-faire* and *laisser-passer*. *Laisser-faire* refers to the functioning of free *internal* markets, unfettered by state intervention, and *laisser-passer* to free *external* markets, unencumbered by custom duties and commercial policies. In both cases the minimum state is prescribed under the assumption that state intervention distorts economic forces and introduces artificial inefficiencies in the functioning of markets. As Adam Smith put it himself:

"It is the highest impertinence and presumption of kings and ministers to pretend to watch over the economy of private people and to restrain their expense either by sumptuary laws or by prohibiting the importation of foreign luxuries. They are, themselves, always and without any exceptions the greatest spendthrifts in the society. Let them look after their own expenses and they can safely trust other people with theirs. If their own extravagance does not ruin the state, that of their subjects never will." (Adam Smith: *The Wealth of Nations*)

The Minimum State thesis incorporated in the Smithian ideology has, however, given rise since to theoretical challenges in the light of a number of market failures under the aegis of capitalism. Thus, alternative schools of thought have arisen, co-existing with the classical school: six of the most prominent among these are reviewed, in approximate chronological order, to shed light on the controversy.

The Marxian-Socialist Challenge

The Marxian-Socialist challenge emerged as the result of the social trauma of the British Industrial Revolution. Writing in the second half of the nineteenth century, Marx and his followers focused on the development of capitalism, on its strengths and weaknesses and on its long-term prognosis. The vitality of capitalism as a wealth-producing progressive force was never challenged by Marx and, in fact, was confirmed by him in numerous passages of both *Das Kapital* and *The Communist Manifesto*. Capitalism was seen as a significant improvement on feudalism and the bourgeois entrepreneur as a highly productive agent. To be to the 'left', or 'progressive', in feudal times would have required being a capitalist. As Marx put it :

"... The bourgeoisie has been the first to show what Man's activity can bring about. It has accomplished wonders far surpassing the Egyptian pyramids, Roman aqueducts and Gothic cathedrals... The bourgeoisie, during its rule of scarce one hundred years, has created more massive and colossal productive forces than have all the previous generations put together." (*The Communist Manifesto*, 1971 edition, pp. 92-94)

However, according to the Marxian authors, the wealth-producing dynamic of free enterprise capitalism is not matched by its fair distributive ability. In Marx and among his disciples, Rosa Luxembourg, Lenin and others, an inexorable trend towards industrial concentration and imperialist expansion is seen to exist within capitalism. In effect, capitalism is characterized as a system which breeds few winners and many losers and which reinforces the trend towards increasingly unequal income distribution.

This Darwinistic 'survival-of-the-fittest' view of capitalist growth is also echoed in the works of one of the most eloquent apologists of capitalism, the Austrian economist Joseph Schumpeter, who characterized economic progress as 'creative destruction'. The winds of change trim the fat off the economy, with the aid of severe business cycles that eliminate marginal firms. This trimming is ultimately a creative process but it is, nevertheless, highly-Darwinistic, since only the very fit survive and the others are destroyed. Natural selection leads to a more robust society but one where the weak, the defeated and the downtrodden do not really have a place: hence the necessity of state intervention on equity grounds. The state comes in to restore the balance - it protects the weak and allows for a better distribution of wealth.

In the Marxian model, the 'maximum state' is a transitionary phase which is designed to last only until the economy reaches ultimate maturity. In the final affluent society, the state will disappear, since it is no longer needed. The 'maximum state' in the form of a command economy is, in the Marxian school of thought, a response to scarcity. Once scarcity is eliminated through economic growth, the state withers away into nothingness and natural forces take over. Thus the ultimate stage of communism does not involve a heavy-handed state but, like the ultimate stage of capitalism, it involves no state at all.

In a nutshell, the principal argument underlying the Marxian critique of the minimum state is the *unsatisfactory distribution* of wealth under conditions of scarcity. Accordingly, socialist governments, especially in European countries, have focused state-intervention more on the problem of distribution and redistribution than on the production of wealth itself.

The Keynesian Challenge

The Keynesian challenge defends a 'non-minimum' state rather than a maximum one. John Maynard Keynes' arguments centred around the presumed failure of markets to maintain the level of effective demand necessary to sustain full employment. In some senses, the Keynesian doctrine is a counterpoint to the Marxian. Whereas the latter claims that the state must intervene under conditions of scarcity, the Keynesian model maintains that the state is needed under conditions of *affluence* in order to stimulate a lazy private sector.

Keynes' *General Theory of Employment, Interest and Money* was published in 1936, in the midst of the Great Depression. It has been viewed by some as the final attempt to reform a dying capitalism and by others as the prelude to socialism. The basic Keynesian model posits a possible difference between actual and potential national demand, a difference that is explainable by the operation of money markets. Liquidity preference leads to hoarding and a low effective demand. In turn, this leads to production at less than full capacity and unemployment. In order to prod the economy back into capacity production, the state must intervene regularly to create the effective demand that the private sector is unable or unwilling to create. To achieve this additional demand, direct government spending over and above revenues, i.e. a *deliberate fiscal deficit,* and/or monetary expansion are needed. Consequently, the state must have counter-cyclical responsibilities and use the tools at its disposal to correct the intrinsic weakness of the market mechanisms.

The Galbraithian Challenge

The Galbraithian challenge is a post-Keynesian intellectual development to be found in the theories of John

Kenneth Galbraith, as outlined in his *Affluent Society* and especially in *The New Industrial State*.

The Galbraithian case against the 'minimum state' is based on alleged market imperfections which render inoperative the ideal of perfect competition, the perennial example of market efficiency. Perfect competition gives way to monopolies or at least oligopolies. Most contemporary industries, claims Galbraith, are characterized either by imperfect competition or by oligopoly. This industrial concentration breeds upon itself and engenders an additional face-off between Big Business and Big Labour. In order to protect society as a whole, Big Government is needed occasionally to impose wage and price controls and apply 'countervailing power', in order to limit the power of free market-generated monopolies. To summarize then, because the 'New Industrial State' is not characterized by free markets but by highly oligopolistic ones, the virtues of free competition are absent and are replaced by monopolistic distortions. The state must intervene to correct these wrongs.

The Development Challenge

The Development challenge is not identified with any one champion: it stems from a general contemporary concern with economic and social development. 'Development' is economic growth with appropriate institutional change. Free market forces alone cannot, according to some theories, generate the momentum necessary for sustained development. The operation of free markets, even perfectly competitive ones, tends to be oriented towards short-term gain, whereas development is a long-term process. Consequently, state intervention is required to create the conditions for such long-term balanced growth.

For instance, it is argued that expensive infrastructural investments are best undertaken by the state. Because of the very long pay-back time of say, railway construction, it has been claimed that no railway would ever have been built in the nineteenth century without some state support, direct or indirect. To some extent this is, in fact, true. There were, indeed, very few instances of completely private railway construction in the nineteenth century. Even the most non-interventionist governments, like those of Britain or the United States, provided at the very least loan guarantees or, in the American case, land grants to spur railway construction.

A further argument in favour of state intervention is that it is necessary in order to achieve balanced regional growth, a high priority concern in a large country like Canada. In this country, it is plausible to assume that with a 'minimum state', market forces would tend to concentrate the great bulk of economic activity in Ontario and deplete the peripheral provinces. The ideal of balanced regional development, an unchallenged axiom of Canadian politics, therefore, militates against the 'minimum state'.

The Environmental Challenge

Concern with environmental quality, the threat of depletion of non-renewable resources and the dangers of pollution have put ecologists in the camp against the 'minimum state'. Since ecological concerns began to interest the public, as a result of the 1972 Club of Rome Report on the *Limits to Growth* , the dangers of a purely market-based management of the physical environment have been noted. At the centre of the debate is the question of 'externalities' - positive benefits or negative nuisances which are by-products of economic activity and which escape the internal cost accounting of the firm.

Pollution, for instance, is the responsibility of everyone, and therefore of no one.

Thomas Malthus had pointed out, in the eighteenth century, that if things were left to themselves, human beings would overpopulate the earth and degrade the environment until unpleasant corrective mechanisms would restore the balance. A market-based management of environmental quality would allow price signals alone to govern such things as pollution and the depletion of non-renewable resources. Consequently, Malthusian mechanisms such as disease, famine and war would be necessary methods to correct imbalances. In order to prevent such damage rather than to correct it after the damage had been done, state intervention would be needed.

The Neo-Mercantilist Challenge

The Mercantilist challenge is both the oldest and the newest challenge to the 'minimum state' thesis. It is the oldest challenge because mercantilist thinking pre-dated Adam Smith and, in fact, served as the principal target for his theories. When Smith started his 'inquiry into the nature and causes of the wealth of nations', it was precisely to counter the then popular view that the pursuit of wealth was a zero-sum game involving the accumulation of gold and silver bullion. On the contrary, argued Smith, wealth is made up of goods and services and its creation is not a zero-sum activity. Smith's claim was that everyone can benefit from free trade, whereas in mercantilist theories, free trade is supposed to breed winners and losers.

The classical school of economics, founded by Adam Smith, never completely buried mercantilism. It co-existed with it. The nineteenth and twentieth centuries have been punctuated by waves of economic liberalism, expressing themselves in free trade agreements and promises of non-interventionism by the state, alternating with regular returns to mercantilist policies. On the European continent, mercantilism has thrived, even when lip-service was paid to free trade. France, Germany, Russia, Sweden, Italy all have long and uninterrupted histories of state interventionism, in some form or other, and so have most other countries on the Continent. In fact, this generalization could be extended to the rest of the world. The economically liberal countries have been few and far between.

Generally, a country will choose the ideal of *laisser-passer* - no custom duties or commercial policies and a truly free trade - when it believes it has overwhelming comparative advantage. Thus, as we have seen in an earlier chapter, Britain abolished the Corn Laws at the height of its Industrial Revolution. It embarked on a free trade experiment based on the belief that it could buy food abroad by exporting industrial goods in large numbers. But Britain's economic liberalism and reliance on international free trade were only partially emulated by its commercial partners.

Today, Japan and the Southeast Asian "NICs" (Newly-Industrialising Countries) are officially in favour of free trade (at least in terms of the elimination of visible *tariff* barriers), because they believe they possess overwhelming comparative advantage in most industrial sectors. When, however, a country feels weak, it will usually resort to protectionist measures.

In the context of the 1990s, the question that must be raised is "How 'free' will the international economy be?"

The most successful economies in the world, today, are those who, like Japan and the Asian NICs, have honed neo-mercantilism into a fine art. The precepts of Jean-

Baptiste Colbert, the Intendant of Louis XIV who developed and refined the French theory of mercantilism, have been the implicit underlying 'bible' not only of French and European *dirigisme*, but more interestingly, of Japanese industrial strategy.

In particular, the judicious use of private sector firms, as state co-ordinated weapons in a global struggle for economic supremacy, is common both to contemporary Japan and Colbert's seventeenth-century France.

In the seventeenth century, state-created monopolies such as the Hudson's Bay Company and the East India Company on the British side and the *Compagnie des Habitants* and the *Compagnie des Indes Orientales* on the French side, were instructed to "advance like armies" to use Colbert's terms and seek economic advantage for the state. Is there not a family resemblance with the thrusts of Toyota, Mitsubishi and Sony in world markets, aided and abetted by a solicitous MITI (Ministry of International Trade and Industry).

If world trade is not free but governed by neo-mercantilist manoeuvres (ranging from hidden subsidies to non-tariff barriers posing as environmental protection laws), is there a likelihood that a 'minimum state', practicing free trade and non-intervention, will have a chance to survive cut-throat international competition? The question remains relevant and makes the neo-mercantilist challenge perhaps the strongest single challenge to the 'minimum state' theory in the nineties.

The Contemporary Version of the Minimum State Thesis.

The contemporary version of the 'minimum state' thesis is based on an updating of the classical Smithian doctrine in monetarist terms and an emphasis on the revealed inefficiency of the 'maximum state' of the seventies, with its undesirable by-products, the 'British disease' of deficits and debt. Underlying that view is the belief that governments can never be as efficient as the private sector in production, distribution or consumption.

One particularly telling point is the waste generated by governments. The structure of fiscal year budget planning, for instance, has as an unintended, but very real, consequence the promotion of waste. There is no incentive for a civil servant to save part of his allocated budget. If he has not spent it all by the fateful March 31 deadline, (which is the end of the fiscal year in Canada), he will be doubly punished. Firstly, he will forego the use of the funds in the fiscal year which has expired. Secondly, he will have his budget cut for the next fiscal year. If, on the other hand he is allowed to overspend, he is twice a winner. He has enjoyed the use of additional funds in the first fiscal year, and can legitimately claim a budget increase for the next. In effect, the public sector in Canada, as in most other countries, *functions on a 'reverse bottom line'*.

From the point of view of the civil servant with signing authority, a 'red bottom line' is a signal to possible expansion of the activities he controls, whereas a 'black bottom line' is almost surely the prelude to involuntary contraction. As one observer has noted, the system forces civil servants to measure their influence and their status by three variables: the budgets they control, the number of people they have working under them and the persons in high places they have access to. All three indicators lead to the same optimum strategy: *spend more*. In other words, independently of the good intentions which underlie most government actions (and we might as well assume good intentions throughout the system) the reward structure is biased in favour of waste. As a result, cross-subsidies, a large bureaucracy, inefficient duplication of services and the ballooning of budgets lead into the spiral of the parasitic 'maximum state' and present the best arguments for the updated version of state 'minimization'.

Anorexia Nervosa: The Perils of Indiscriminate Downsizing

In the early eighties, a number of Western governments decided to peremptorily 'downsize' the state, adopting strategies that were politically palatable but not carefully thought-out. In Canada and the United States these have involved five areas:
• deficit and debt reduction through spending cuts;
• tax reduction;
• privatization and de-regulation;
• a reduction in *visible* industrial policy supports;
• an attempted relaxation of protectionist policies

Spending Cuts

The attempt to downsize on the spending side has been largely unsuccessful. So far, it has been tackled with the kind of misguided zeal shown by the overweight individual who wishes to become slim again overnight, and develops anorexia nervosa! Taking weight reduction as a suitable metaphor, let us note that it was mistakenly believed, for a long time, that physical weight was just a matter of calorie counting. Yet more subtle analysis revealed that simple calorie counting, which does not take into account the complexities of biochemical interactions in the body, has little chance of succeeding as a weight control. The contemporary thinking on the subject is that to lose weight one must act on the body's metabolism. In fact, modern theories on the question favour changing the 'set-point' of the equilibrium weight (which apparently every individual possesses), in order to achieve permanent weight control. If that set-point, often psychological, is not changed, then skipping meals will just increase appetite further and the weight loss will, at best, be temporary. The anorexic may alternate between gorging and starvation with, as a net result, great harm to his or her health.

Applying this metaphor to government activities, one can claim that *unless the functions of government are revised and, when required, replaced by alternative activities undertaken by the private sector, indiscriminate minimization of government activity will do more harm than good.* It will weaken the body-politic and de-stabilize the private sector.

For instance, sudden cuts in government contracts might lead to massive lay-offs in that part of the private sector dependent on those contracts. The state cuts its contract-spending only to acquire new responsibilities in the form of the higher unemployment. It then hastens to put in place wasteful make-work programmes or, alternatively, 'dishes out' unemployment compensation. The result is that, ultimately, more money is spent than saved. On the whole, the 1980s' record of attempted spending cuts has been one of form and not of substance.

In Britain, attempts to reduce the fiscal deficit were undertaken under the Thatcher regime, partially through the sale of government-owned enterprises. This de-nationalization process was aimed at correcting the mistakes of the previous Labour governments. The principal objective was to reduce the PSBR (Public Sector Borrowing Requirement) which has been at the heart of

Britain's fiscal policy for the last ten years. However, the reduction in the PSBR was achieved with a countervailing increase of the PSFD - the Public Sector Financial Deficit!

A careful management of the deficit must incorporate the notion of 'net worth'. If government were to be run like a business, the 'flogging' of public assets and the 'blowing' of North Sea oil revenues, which have reduced the net worth of the nation, would be severely reprimanded rather than praised.

As far as the United States is concerned, public spending did not decrease, but increased massively. The 1981 U.S. budget deficit was $80 billion. By 1986, a complacent Congress had allowed budget deficits two to three times as large. The National Debt doubled and interest payments reached $150 billion a year in 1986. As far as the external deficit is concerned, in 1981, the balance of payments of the United States was in surplus. In 1986, it had a $150 billion deficit. The Reagan experiment with state-minimization amounted, on the spending side, to the financing of a huge military build-up with borrowed money. As an editorial in the *New York Herald Tribune* noted: "For all the heavy breathing, the only thing the President and Congress have done about the twin towers of debt is to allow them to grow higher than ever."

The U.S federal debt increased substantially in the Reagan years and the ratio of interest payments to government expenditures reached 13 percent. The debt-to-GNP ratio has, however, remained relatively constant, varying between 44 percent in 1966 and 49 percent in 1985. The fiscal deficit has been compounded by a balance of payments deficit which has worsened the international debt problem. One of the critical questions of the seventies was the management of inflation. A critical question of the eighties and probably the nineties is the management of the U.S. trade deficits. Between 1919 and 1982, the United States was a net creditor. In 1988, it was the largest single debtor on earth.

As far as Canada is concerned, the Canadian fiscal debt has not decreased in the recent past, but has increased more slowly since the Conservatives came to office in 1984. The federal government has brought down its rate of increase of spending in 1984-1986 to the lowest rate since World War II. In spite of that fact, it was higher by 40 percent in 1986 than in 1984. However, debt has risen more slowly than GNP.

Tax revenues, as percentage of GNP, was 18 percent in 1970 and 17 percent in 1986. We 'put the cap' on taxes. However, the debt/GNP ratio remains very high. Among the OECD countries, only Italy has a higher debt/GNP ratio than Canada. Canadian foreign indebtedness in 1975 was $30 billion. In 1986, it was $130 billion. Foreign debt service was 20 percent of export earnings.

In sum then, the attempts to reduce the deficit through spending reductions have not been successful, so far, and are unlikely to be more so in the future. Above and beyond the economic constraints on further reductions in state spending, (a recession might force government spending to increase once again for contra-cyclical reasons) there are also political constraints. The social policies of the seventies have created entitlement groups wielding strong political power; these groups will not easily accept having their benefits curtailed. The aged, among others, will insist on social security benefits and health costs will continue to stay high. When confronted with the reality of pressure groups with political clout, all democratic governments tend to beat a hasty retreat - or find themselves out of office the next time around. The Conservatives retreated on universality in 1985. Similarly, the Quebec government retreated on the issue of increased tuition fees, in 1986, when it was revealed that it would cost the government many popularity points. The Chirac government, in France, also backed down on the issue of a partial privatization of education, when students took to the streets and threatened the political survival of the rightist regime. It seems that everyone is for deficit reduction, as long as it will not mean a direct sacrifice involved for the group to which one belongs.

It is worthwhile pointing out that one of the entitlement groups in Canada is made-up of the *provincial governments* on the receiving end of federal equalization payments. These governments will not accept massive reductions of federal transfer payments without putting strong pressure on the central government - if necessary, they will revive, with a vengeance, the federal/provincial confrontations of the 1970s. The political influence of the provinces further decreases the likelihood of success of massive spending reductions by the federal government.

Tax Reduction

While spending cuts seem to have been going nowhere, income tax reduction appears to have a more promising future. The U.S. tax reform, of 1986, has paved the way for what may become a worldwide revolution in direct taxation. It represents an outstanding success for the 'minimum state'. The United States chose to eliminate many tax breaks and reduce direct taxation. By 1988, the highest U.S. personal income tax rate was 28 percent, as compared with Quebec's 60 percent.

The reduction in personal tax rates must be followed by similar changes in Canada; otherwise, it will give too great an advantage to the United States - especially in the context of free trade in services. A 'brain drain' in favour of the United States would deplete Canada of valuable factors of production. Two difficulties, however, remain. The U.S. tax reform is supposed to be revenue neutral. It will be financed by the closing of existing tax loopholes. There are fewer tax loopholes to close in Canada and, in addition, whatever tax breaks do exist are often a provincial responsibility and cannot be abolished by the federal government. Consequently, although income tax reductions are probably inevitable in Canada, in the long run they are not likely to be as revenue neutral as in the United States. This will compound the difficulties of resolving the deficit problem.

Above and beyond the U.S initiative in tax reform, there seem to be strong reasons why taxation rates, especially at the personal level, must go down.

One of them is the rise of the informal economy, which accounts for between 10 percent and 35 percent of the GDP in the OECD countries. The informal economy reduces the tax base as producers and consumers resort to barter deals and self-consumption to avoid what has become a punitive tax system. If taxation rates are increased, this will further drive activity to the underground economy. There is a limit to what the taxpayer will accept and this limit has, in the opinion of many observers, already been reached.

One form of taxation which may expand is indirect taxation (sales taxes and value-added taxes). It is easier to tax the uses of income than its sources and the effects are less perceptible. The sales tax can be buried in the cost of the product, with no competitive disadvantage to home producers and a certain invisibility to consumers. In many European countries, taxes are hidden in the final price of products and remain unnoticed by consumers who are not particularly interested in the components of the price they are faced with in the store. What goes to rent, what goes to labour and what goes to taxes is the store owner's problem. Consumers have the problem of deciding whether they are getting value for money and they can do that more easily when the price includes the taxes than when it does not.

Another argument against increased direct taxation is the enormous cost it involves. If all the support systems are accounted for, the redistribution of national income through taxation is a particularly inefficient method. The cost of redistribution itself may absorb almost 25 percent of what is raised.

Privatization and Deregulation

Privatization, or the sale of state-owned enterprises to the private sector in order to reduce the size of the public sector, has been proceeding in many countries and is currently very much in vogue. However, there is some evidence that the early enthusiasm for that particular form of state-minimization is waning, for reasons which will be elaborated in a later section of this chapter.

Deregulation has proceeded in the United States since the late seventies and a number of other countries are experimenting with it. However, like privatization, some of the enthusiasm for it is waning and the reviews are mixed concerning the success of the already deregulated industries. Many now believe that deregulation leads to *unregulated oligopoly* and not free competition. It is not at all obvious whether the public interest is, indeed, better served by these unregulated oligopolies.

A classical case-study of deregulation is the airline industry. Airline deregulation, in the United States, has led to some positive results, such as a fall in the price of tickets by about 20 percent in real terms. However, it was accompanied by a reduction in the quality of services offered to consumers and an apparent reduction in safety standards. The United States Federal Aviation Agency had 2,000 inspectors to monitor 237 carriers in 1979. In 1984, it had 1,300 inspectors to monitor 407 carriers. Out of 43 carriers investigated in 1984, 13 were fined. Deregulation, in the United States, also forced strict economies on many non-American carriers. Before 1979, metal fatigue and corrosion were responsible for 21.4 percent of all crashes. Four years following deregulation the figure jumped to 38.7 percent. The age of the airline fleet in 1971 was five years. In 1985 it was ten. As Michael Ramsdan asserted in *Flight International:*

> There is no doubt that safety standards are falling. In the eyes of professionals, deregulation is reducing safety margins. It is a very subtle form of incapacitation that statistics cannot fully measure. You do not get obvious violations, just little failures to do better than minimum standards and, as soon as you start doing that, you can get some very bad accidents.

Twenty-nine percent of Canadian GDP is subject to regulation as to prices, entry or output. Although deregulation is being experimented with at different levels in Canada, there is a suspicion that what may appear as deregulation may end up as *re-regulation*. New regulatory bodies, such as provincial governments, may replace the old and failing that, mergers and cartels may privately regulate what was hitherto regulated by the state.

Laisser-faire vs. Industrial Policy

The concept of an 'industrial policy' is antithetical to the 'minimum state' philosophy. Both the Reagan administration, in 1981, and the Conservative government in Canada, in 1984, temporarily banished the notion from their political vocabulary. Even France, a traditional leader in industrial policy has, under the Chirac Government, retreated from the notion. However, once again there is evidence that most countries pursue covert neo-mercantilism, despite the lip-service paid to the abolition of industrial policies and to the notion that the private sector should be left to develop on its own.

The world leaders in industrial policy are, of course the Japanese and their Asian emulators, South Korea, Taiwan, Hong Kong and Singapore. Apart from the legendary Ministry of International Trade and Industry and the long-term guidance it gives the Japanese economy, more specific policy instruments exist to help the private sector achieve economic objectives deemed desirable by the state. The results speak for themselves. Japan is now the most affluent industrial nation on earth, having recently surpassed the United States in per capita income.

As far as the NICs are concerned, their industrial policies are supplemented by straight exchange-rate manipulations, reminiscent of the bullion accumulation policies of the early mercantilists. From February 1985 to December 1986, the yen and German mark went up 60 and 70 percent respectively against the U.S. dollar. Yet, the Hong Kong dollar remains pegged since 1983. Taiwan and South Korea have opted for managed floats, with the emphasis on 'managed'. Since February 1985, the Taiwan dollar has gone up 9 percent against the U.S. dollar, while the South Korean one has gone down 2 percent. The result has been huge trade surpluses. Taiwan's trade surplus is 20 percent of GNP, while Japan's is only 4 percent. Taiwan foreign exchange reserves, in December 1986, were $44 billion or the second largest in the world. Taiwan and South Korean markets remain sheltered behind tariff walls.

Countries that do not have a neo-mercantilist reputation, nevertheless, use mercantilist practices. The British government participates in the private sector through joint ventures. The German approach is 'hands-off' unless needed.

A Kiel Institute study on the German economy confirms, however, strong mercantilist policies. Germany is still hooked on exports and will do whatever is necessary to promote them. But state intervention is more subtle than in the NICs and often occurs at the level of the 'Länder' instead of that of the federal government. Whatever the future of West Germany (which is experimenting with downsizing like everyone else), the past superlative economic performance of the Federal Republic was achieved with subsidies, regulation, mercantilist policies and state participation in private sector activities - not with a 'minimum state'.

The United States approach to industrial policy under the Reagan administration has been to deny its existence - and yet to exercise it through procurement policies centred around two long-term mega-projects: Defence and NASA. The enormous budget deficits, which have stimulated the American economy and fuelled its recent expansion, have been described by some observers as 'disguised Keynesianism'. The military build-up and the Strategic Defence Initiative may fuel private sector growth for decades to come, if maintained at projected levels. One way or the other, it is a far cry from state minimization.

In Canada, the ill-fated and aborted 'industrial strategy' debate of the seventies ("Canada has an industrial strategy, but the rest of the world has industries") has placed this issue on the 'back burner' at the federal level. Provincial industrial strategies thrive, nevertheless, and typically take the form of non-tariff trade barriers and incentive and procurement policies.

Laisser-passer vs Protectionism

Free trade with the United States, or in other words the 'minimization of the state's intervention in commercial policy', has been Canada's official medium-term objective since 1985. Yet, once again, we have a gap between statements of intention and actual behaviour. Between 1985 and 1987, 'free trade' gradually became 'freer trade' or 'enhanced trade' on the Canadian side - while on the U.S. side, the headlines reported new countervailing duties and rumbles of protectionism from the U.S. Congress throughout the summer of 1987. With non-tariff trade barriers, national procurement policies, the subtle manipulation of taxation, and hidden subsidies, international trade is only nominally-free and the hand of the state is visible enough to the practiced eye behind the Smithian 'invisible hand'. As was noted in earlier chapters, the final implementation of the 1989 Free Trade Accord between the two countries will not necessarily mean the removal of non-tariff barriers on either side. State intervention will still be present, but now more hidden.

For all these reasons one cannot say, with confidence, that the 'minimum state' is with us. Even if it were deemed to be fully desirable, it is not likely to come about anytime soon. There are too many economic, political and social constraints to allow it to become a reality. Yet, the 'maximum state' of the seventies is equally bankrupt. How do we then escape from the dilemma? What is needed is original thinking about a number of intermediate models between the extreme formulae of 'gorging' and 'starvation'. The theory of the 'optimum state' is in its infancy. We would propose that the final section of this chapter serve as a preface to the elaboration of such a theory.

Rethinking the State in the Nineties: Managing Complexity

The current and future predicament of governments may be succinctly stated as follows: *The state's level of responsibility will not decrease and is, in fact, likely to increase; yet the means of financing the discharge of these responsibilities through conventional methods have reached a ceiling.* In particular, taxation cannot be counted-on as a method for the further funding of an expansionary state - and neither can borrowing. What then is the solution? The temptation to inflate their way out of trouble may be irresistible for hard-pressed governments, but the long-term consequences of such a strategy will be counterproductive. By a process of elimination, we come to what may become the blueprint for future government financing: *productive activity yielding a surplus.*

Such an approach will appear heretical to some. In one sense it implies a 'privatization' of government, not in the sense of selling-off public assets to the private sector but of adopting some of the governing principles of private sector management within the public sector. This will inevitably be opposed by those who believe, on ideological grounds, that governments should never function in a private sector mode. In another sense, a productive public sector implies a direct incursion in the traditional preserve of the private sector and will be resisted by others who believe, on opposing ideological grounds, that governments have no business competing with the private sector. But if the Scylla of a 'maximum state', financed by heavy taxes, and the Charybdis of an 'anemic state' unable to manage the complexity of governance, are to be avoided, intermediate solutions will have to be considered.

The 'management of social complexity' is, in fact, the principal challenge facing present and future governments. Socio-economic environments are getting more and more turbulent as technological change is accelerating. Progress is achieved through Schumpeterian 'creative destruction'. Winners and losers emerge from this process and unless one is to court explosive class struggle between them, this turbulence must be managed, defused, and ultimately harnessed.

Potentially strong economic growth lies ahead for the world economy because of the proliferation of technological multipliers. The generic technologies of informatics, bio-technologies, communications, transportation, energy and synthetic materials are ushering in a new industrial revolution which is changing the production function.

Output has the capability to increase massively. But this output will require fewer inputs; and among the inputs likely to be 'economized' is labour itself. This will, inevitably, affect the pattern of distribution. New roles will emerge for the state, only some of which are presently imaginable. Yet these new roles will have to be envisioned, given the financial predicament created by the dilemma of increased responsibilities and reduced means to deliver them.

As a preface to the theory of the 'optimum state', let us put forward three ideas for change: 1. a 'productive' public sector; 2. a 'socially responsible' private sector; and 3. a growing organic relationship between the two.

1. A Productive Public Sector

Should the public sector be intrinsically productive and should its products be offered for sale to its clients, or should it merely be an instrument for transfer payments? What governments produce has, traditionally, been different from what the private sector produces, but this distinction is, increasingly, being blurred. Many of the functions performed by government are being considered for privatization and are, indeed, being transferred to the private sector. The reverse process is equally plausible and some private sector production could be taken over by the government. The purpose of this reverse transfer from private to public sector would be twofold. First, it would guarantee that certain collective goods, presently not offered by the private sector, would be provided (for example, infrastructure or public goods with high external economies but low internal economies). Second, it would give the government a source of financing separate from taxes.

This line of thinking may shed a completely new light on the whole privatization movement. First, there is the revenue dimension. A productive and, indeed, profitable public sector would require that it should get rid of its 'dog' programmes, which could be better managed in the private sector, but keep its 'milk cows' to finance its growing responsibilities. At the limit, it should even acquire new 'milk cows' from the private sector or create them from scratch. The experience of governments who do not have to depend on taxes to finance their activities, in this connection, is quite interesting. Oil-producing states, like some of the OPEC countries, Texas and Alberta (when oil prices were high), gambling havens like Monaco, or banking havens like Switzerland, generally provide high levels of public services, without imposing crippling burdens on the private sector.

The state with independent means can allow the nation to 'have its cake and eat it too'. The downside, of course, is that taxation brings with it accountability, while independent financing may lead to corruption and excesses. However, this need not necessarily be so. The private sector's non-dependence on taxes does not lead it, inevitably, into exploitation and corruption. There is a certain degree of self-discipline necessary in both cases; however, there is more danger of abuse from an uncontrolled private monopoly than from a democratically-elected government, even if it were to enjoy more independent means.

The second point relating to privatization concerns the oft-made assertion that market forces allocate resources best and that government bodies are congenitally inefficient. This assertion is based on a comparison of economic *theory* with the *practice* of government mismanagement. It is not, however, based on actual market practice. In fact, if one were to oppose ideal public management with actual market practice, one might get very different results. There are many examples where well-run public enterprises defeat their private counterparts. The Swiss National Railways have, over the years, been a model of efficiency which shames many private-sector carriers in North America. From 1975 to 1986, the public sector Soviet and Czech national hockey teams have regularly defeated and sometimes humiliated the National Hockey League private sector professionals, in spite of the latter's large salaries and 'perks'.

There are public sector successes and private sector failures which, in effect, depend on the appropriateness of the management techniques employed. Market failures are often due to imperfections, externalities and the short-run orientation of competitive players who cannot afford to 'play' the long run. In a highly competitive market, in the long run, we are all dead. Yet, today's social complexity may require long-term thinking beyond what private bodies may consider. Similarly, public-sector failures are often attributable to lack of incentive, poor management, faulty business intelligence and counter-productive rules.

Ultimately, the question of the motivation and reward structures of senior management is paramount. Human beings are driven by greed, by love, by hate, fear, compassion and sex. Reward systems are essential for motivation (whether the reward is in this or another world). The capitalist market system is a superb motivator and driver for achievement, but is it the only one? The monetary rewards obtainable in the free market are valuable incentives for better performance, but they are already gravely diminished by the taxation system that 'gives with one hand and takes away with the other'.

In addition, one must not forget the incentive power of non-monetary rewards. Prestige, recognition, power and other less-tangible, yet very real, reward systems can be strong motivators. The Army and the Church have used such rewards since early history.

In fact, even in the private sector, beyond a certain threshold, executives are motivated much more by the intangibles or the 'perks' associated with their jobs, including job satisfaction, than the monetary rewards which are, of necessity, subject to the laws of diminishing returns.

Public enterprise is an important feature of many successful economies in the world. The importance of public enterprises is highest in Austria, surprisingly quite low in Japan and in between in Canada. The German state has holdings of over 25 percent in almost 500 German companies, 25 percent in Volkswagen and 25 percent in VEBA, the energy conglomerate. If these are added to the state's majority holdings, they create a private annex of 500,000 employees. The use of state co-ordinated conglomerates has been a central feature of both German and Japanese industrial strategies. The Canadian experience has not been as successful, largely because the Crown corporations have unclear and occasionally self-contradictory missions; this may demoralize the senior management who long to be completely privately owned.

If the state is to be productive, not only should it possess a number of 'milk cows', but its overall performance should be lean and waste-free. In order to achieve this result, new operating rules have to be introduced in the civil service. At least five factors favour waste in government spending and should be dealt with, if government is to become more productive:

• Vague performance indicators. It is very difficult to measure the actual performance of a public servant other than by the intellectually-incestuous peer review process. Consequently, input indicators (salaries and spending levels) masquerade as output indicators and promote waste.

• The reverse bottom-Line approach of zero-based budgeting unintentionally promotes over-spending since there is no incentive to create surpluses. Unused budgets are lost, therefore spending and over-spending is rational.

• The politics of the civil service promotes 'empire-building' at taxpayers' expense. If success in the civil service could be measured in other ways, there would be less incentive for every department head and sub-head to want to expand.

• Inter-departmental and inter-governmental rivalry leads to cross-subsidies and inefficiency. An alarming number of programmes in the federal, provincial and municipal governments duplicate each other.

• Contradictory government objectives bring confusion into the system. Cost reduction almost always takes the form of lay-offs and unemployment. Yet, the government is committed to creating jobs and often will resort to completely artificial and wasteful 'make-work' programmes. It cuts on one side and overspends on the other.

The theory of the Productive Public Sector also has implications concerning 'good' and 'bad' deficits. What is a good deficit? Korea and Argentina have the same ratios of debt to GNP, yet most observers will worry about Argentina and not about Korea. The Japanese government deficit is immense, yet is no cause for alarm. It is worthwhile noting that deficits are not the monopoly of the public sector. There are large private sector deficits, balance of payments deficits and what environmentalists call 'ecological deficits', structural ecological imbalances brought about by human action. Japanese corporations are much more leveraged than those in the United States, yet this is no cause for concern. However, in all areas private or public, a 'good' deficit is one which satisfies at least one of the following conditions:

a) It is a *temporary* deficit that is used to accumulate capital and that will eventually lead to large future surpluses. In this sense, private citizens and businesses have large deficits which they absorb by future production.

b)It is a *permanent but sectoral* deficit which actually boosts performance in other sectors so that the net effect is very positive. This happens, for instance, when government spending generates strong economic activity, or when investment in infrastructure pays off in indirect ways by promoting better performance from individual productive agents.

This second condition, in effect, entails that spillovers, external economies and indirect effects will make the deficit worthwhile. By way of example, in 1944, the Canadian fiscal deficit was 22 percent of GDP. This is considerably higher than contemporary deficits but was justified by the "investment in victory" idea. In addition, the Canadian economy, in 1944, enjoyed full employment, generated a very large national income and possessed stable prices.

2. A Socially Responsible Private Sector.

In the same way that the public sector should 'privatize' its thinking, private sector thinking should, ideally, become more socially responsible. This implies that the private objectives of profit maximization should be tempered by a consideration of external economies and dis-economies and a general underlying concern for the public good. As the private sector becomes more socially responsible, the public sector's functions will, correspondingly, decrease.

One area where this social responsibility is particularly relevant is employment. Large Japanese firms have the reputation of maintaining a policy of permanent employment for their labour forces even when the dictates of profit-maximization would recommend downsizing. This creates a sense of trust and security that is translated into higher quality of goods and services and more productivity.

The employment question will remain at the top of the public policy agenda because there is increasing belief that the private sector will not create enough jobs to employ everyone - not because of an economic failure but because of great technological progress that allows more to be done with less. This raises the question of technological unemployment, discussed further in the next chapter.

Insofar as the private sector is either unable or unwilling to assume a responsibility for employment above and beyond its own profit-maximization requirements, the state will have to intervene. At the limit, it will have to employ workers directly and channel them into lucrative productive activities which are revenue-bearing.

State employment is, today, quite high in the world. The mean figure for OECD countries is 18.4 percent of the labour force, with a high of 31.8 percent in Sweden and a surprising low in Japan of 6.6 percent. The Japanese government employs fewer people because of the excellent partnership it has with the private sector, making massive direct employment unnecessary.

3.Towards an Organic Partnership

The management of contemporary environmental turbulence requires that the public and private sectors, in any one country, view each other not as adversaries but as partners. The domain of this partnership will vary with each country, but some kind of common national development will have to be identified and implemented.

Adversarial relations between the two sectors and between labour and management weaken the international competitive potential of a society and make it ungovernable. History is full of examples of the decline of hitherto strong nations when the social consensus was destroyed, and the rise of hitherto peripheral ones when a new social consensus was created.

Japan's rise after the Meiji Restoration in the mid-nineteenth century is a classical example of the immense impetus a new social consensus can bring about. Before the Meiji Restoration and for many centuries, strife and adversarial confrontations, within Japan, sapped the energies of that island nation and confined it to underdevelopment. The new consensus and the opening to the West changed that and allowed Japan to embark upon its meteoric rise.

The public/private partnership in Canada has had a checkered history. In its heyday, it has established the nation's integral links, mobilized capital in two world wars and created the basis for an industrial infrastructure. At its nadir, it has spawned a confrontation economy that has prevented the full blossoming of Canadian entrepreneurs, forcing them to move south in order to bring their ideas to fruition. The public/private adversary system has, in the seventies, added an even more severe federal/provincial face-off, which has become a quasi-perennial feature of Canadian politics. These two institutional adversary systems have taken a heavy toll and reduced the country's performance.

Yet the experience of the international 'winners', in today's highly competitive world economy, points to team work and close collaboration for international success, together with some degree of indicative planning. Indeed, a new model of the state is arising which goes beyond the minimalist state-as-referee and the maximalist paternalistic state. It is the concept of the *state-as-coach,* which is one possible reading of the Japanese experience. In that concept, the state assumes a low public profile, much like the coach of a football or hockey team, and allows the players to capture the limelight and provide superlative performance. However, behind the scenes, the coach prepares the players, trains them and makes them ready for the international economic olympics.

In this concept, the government expenditure-to-GNP ratio remains relatively low. As Figure 3 indicates, if one were to compare the shares of government in GNP in the United States, Canada and Japan, one would find that the Japanese figure is about the same as that of the United States, but lower than Canada's and than the OECD average. In comparing statist Japan and conservative Britain in 1982, one is surprised to discover a 34.2 percent government expenditure-to-GNP ratio for Japan versus 47.4 percent for the U.K. Japanese governments have managed to be infinitely more effective in inserting themselves as productive forces in the economy, without overwhelming it.

**GOVERNMENT EXPENDITURES
AS PERCENTAGE OF GNP**

COUNTRY	1960-68	1980
United States	28.8	35.3
Japan	19.0	34.5
Canada	29.8	41.0
OECD	29.9	40.0

(*Macdonald Commission Report.* Vol. II, p. 50)

Figure 3

In 1986, the total weight of the public sector in Canada's economy amounted to about 50 percent of the GDP (when provincial and municipal levels of government are counted). However, Canada did not seem to be able to use this weight as effectively as Japan used its one-third. The stimulation of private sector activity, rather than its replacement, is the key idea here.

The 'state-as-coach' idea also features an information-providing and indicative planning function. There is an ideological blindness, in the West, concerning planning which has become a dirty word in the wake of the prevalence of the state-minimization doctrine. What has been the actual record of the past few years? Have the partially planned, totally planned or completely unplanned economies fared best?

The *completely planned* economies have fared worst, including Russia, Eastern Europe and Mao Tse Tsung's China, before that country revised its strategies in the Japanese direction. The *completely unplanned* economies, like Britain, have steadily de-industrialized. Britain has lost one-third of her industry to foreign competition since 1979. The *partially-planned* economies have done best, led by Japan. Whereas North Korea's heavy-handed planning has led to weak economic performance, South Korea's indicative planning has obtained results beyond the planners' expectations. South Korea experimented with American-style zero-planning until 1961, and then adopted Japanese-style planning. Its 1961 per capita income was $80, as compared with $2,000 now. In an ideal system, the state's presence must be light and subtle, rather than heavy and gross.

It follows, then, that the state, in Canada as elsewhere, must be rethought from the ground up. Even

e public and
o a fruitful
een briefly
to the third
ent.

Chapter 7

RETHINKING LABOUR
AFTER INFORMATICS

As we have seen in the two previous chapters, adversarial relations among levels of government and between the public and private sectors impede the full realization of Canada's potential. In this chapter, we will examine Canada's third major adversarial system, the one that opposes management and labour. This is an opposition that has persisted, in spite of the fact that what is needed is a co-operative undertaking to understand and manage creatively a dramatically-changing world of work.

Industrial relations have, traditionally, been strained in North America, and in Canada in particular. For many years, Canada had one of the worst strike records among modern industrial countries, in terms of work days lost. We will examine here the future of the management/labour interface, in the light of the effects of the technological revolution. It will be argued that planning for the future, in this area, will have to be tripartite, rather than unilateral or even bilateral. Labour, management and government will have to co-operate in devising win/win scenarios acceptable to all. Future planning will have to meet the challenge of informatics, the most significant single variable likely to affect the nature of work and of working.

The Uncoupling Hypothesis
From Mechanization to Informediation.

As historians often claim, the most important economic event of modern times was the Industrial Revolution. In fact, industrialization developed through at least three phases. Early in Chapter 3, we traced the progression from the first phase, with its seminal innovation of the steam engine, through the second, with its internal combustion engine, oil, and electricity. We pointed out that nuclear power was eclipsed by information as the heart of the third phase. We return here to the implications of this progression for the future of work.

The first two phases of industrialization had one thing in common. The core innovations were energy-based and their effects on human labour important but not decisive. Human and animal energy were replaced by steam power and, in the second phase, by piston and electrical power. This process could be described as *mechanization,* or the substitution of energy-intensive machines for certain forms of physical labour.

To be sure, the nature of work changed somewhat, but horses and other animals were much more displaced by the machines than human beings were - for a very simple reason: humans have never been very efficient energy-machines. When the machines allowed horsepower to be multiplied, it was the horses that were made redundant, not human beings. Human beings found jobs in the new factories. These jobs were not particularly well-paying, but they were jobs, nevertheless. In fact, mechanization greatly increased the demand for industrial jobs, although it *diminished irreversibly* the need for agricultural jobs. Indeed, mechanization made agriculture much more efficient, increasing the productivity of agricultural workers and, therefore, reducing the need for them.

Mechanization was not the final stage of industrialization. The 1950s marked the beginnings of a third industrial revolution. This time, the key innovations were not energy but information intensive. The revolution was focused on the twin fields of computers and telecommunication. In the forty years since the first ENIAC computer, the technology has been through four generations.

The first generation was based on the technology of vacuum tubes. It was a scientific marvel but an economic failure, because the vacuum tubes were physically enormous, were prone to frequent breakdowns and had very little computing power.

The second generation of computers evolved around the transistor. It reduced the volume of computers, and increased both their reliability and their performance.

By the early seventies, the now ubiquitous micro-chip was invented - a computer processor etched on a microscopic wafer of silicon. This computer-on-a-chip led to quantum jumps in performance, reliability and miniaturization which, in turn, led to widespread applications for the technology.

As miniaturization progressed, generation number three gave way to generation number four, characterized by very large integration of electrical circuits on micro-chips (VLSI). This further increased miniaturization, decreased costs and widened the potential field of applications.

With each improvement, more areas of human endeavour became candidates for computerization such that, today, the list of non-computerable activities is shrinking rapidly. Even so, the technology has continued to progress and is presently at the threshold of the so-called 'fifth generation', which is said to involve artificial intelligence. Computer hardware and software have reached the stage of beginning to emulate what we call intelligence. Although there are sceptics, there is reason to believe that many mental activities, hitherto the monopoly of the human brain, will be able to be simulated on computers. This will further extend the fields of applicability of the technology.

And beyond the fifth generation lies a potential sixth, which will probably not mature until we are well into the twenty-first century, but which may be as significant as the first five put together. This is the generation of the 'biochip' involving the marriage of computer and biotechnology.

Thus, the process which began, in 1780, as 'mechanization' has now given rise to a more advanced trend which Iris Fitzpatrick, of the Gamma Institute, has called 'informediation'.

Informediation, or the mediation of human activity by high technology information machines (computers, satellite dishes, fibre optics), has become more and more pervasive. Whereas the mechanization phases of industrialization only replaced physical energy, informediation has allowed a degree of pervasiveness for the technology which is almost all-encompassing.

Some areas of human intelligence, such as perception, conception and motor co-ordination of activity by the brain, are already simulated either in experimental robots or in advanced laboratory experiments. Already, before even the fifth generation gets up to speed, advanced computers can easily defeat human beings at a number of intellectual operations, including the obvious one of 'computing' itself or 'number-crunching'. The possibility of true artificial intelligence or computer emulation of thinking, which appeared so improbable just a few years ago, is now considered highly plausible. In spite of the immense strides taken so far, the quantum jumps are yet to come, but may be upon us, for good or for ill, in the next two decades.

When 'informediation' crosses the threshold of artificial intelligence what future can we envision for human labour? Who will need it? This is where the 'uncoupling hypothesis' comes in.

Technology and Labour : The Historical Pattern

The 'uncoupling hypothesis' is the proposition that there is a long-term pattern of 'uncoupling' or 'decoupling' of production and human labour. As technology advances, we tend to become more productive and do more with less. One of the things we 'do more with less' is human labour. We need less of it to achieve a given result. Therefore, the argument goes, the demand for labour *will not increase at the same rate as economic growth*. In fact, it may decrease, not because technology has failed us, but rather because it has succeeded too well in this regard.

What historical evidence is there concerning this 'uncoupling' process? First, let us consider the effects of mechanization on the primary sector and, in particular, on agriculture.

A hundred and fifty years ago, a good two-thirds of the North American labour force was engaged in producing enough food to feed itself and the rest of the population. Following mechanization and then the green revolution the situation, today, is quite different. Only about three percent of the labour force is directly engaged in agricultural production, while perhaps another fifteen percent is involved in the agro-business value-chain. This includes the marketing and distribution of the goods - clearly service-oriented activities. The three percent that is responsible for the actual production is sufficient, not only to produce enough food to feed itself and the rest of the population, but also to allow North America to export foodstuffs to many other countries.

Today, most developed areas of the world produce food surpluses while employing only a very small fraction of the labour force. It is quite evident that, for these areas, no conceivable expansion in the demand for food will increase agricultural employment. If we all decide to eat more, production will be increased but without necessitating the hiring of many more workers. As far as modern agriculture is concerned, it would be very difficult to pretend that uncoupling has not occurred.

The uncoupling of production and employment in agriculture has not had traumatic effects on the labour force, because redundant workers moved to the cities and to secondary manufacturing, courtesy of the Industrial Revolution. Now, however, there is mounting evidence that the same uncoupling phenomenon is occurring in manufacturing. The facts show that, although industrial production has increased considerably in the last few decades in North America, the number of blue collar workers employed in this manufacturing has not expanded proportionately.

In fact, the actual trend is towards a reduction in blue collar employment. This is the result of both classical mechanization (highly efficient production lines) and more contemporary informediation. The latter finds expression in computer-assisted design, computer-assisted manufacturing, flexible manufacturing systems and, ultimately, robotics.

No new labour-intensive factories are emerging in the leading industrial countries. The new code-phrase describing the challenge of international competitiveness is 'automate or liquidate'. For instance, if the North American car industry is going to compete successfully with the Asian imports, it is not going to do so by hiring armies of new workers but, on the contrary, by *downsizing* and introducing cost-efficient robots. Furthermore, we are seeing the emergence of flexible manufacturing systems. These are highly automated modular production systems that can shift from the assembly of cars to the assembly of stereos at the touch of a dial, thus further reducing the demand for labour.

If human labour is needed less in agriculture and in industry, where will it go? "It will go to services" is the conventional answer. We are moving towards a 'tertiary' economy, it is argued, one where most of us will earn our livings performing miscellaneous services.

On the face of it, this thesis appears to be supported by historical evidence. The service sector is, indeed, the principal job-creator today. The majority of jobs which are listed by Employment Canada did not exist, even in the most fertile imaginations, twenty-five years ago. Is it not, therefore, reasonable to suppose that the jobs made redundant in agriculture and manufacturing will automatically be replaced by service jobs? If so, technological unemployment is just a question of the retraining necessary to assume these new occupations. Accordingly, the state, management and labour, should get together to ease the transition.

But is this really so? Will the service economy create all the necessary new jobs, or is it liable to experience, in the long run, the same uncoupling phenomenon? The evidence is mixed. It is safe to assume that there will be considerable new activity in the service sector. But it is not obvious that this activity will create masses of new jobs. Consider what is happening every day. Computer software is invented, almost daily, to replace activities which were hitherto human-delivered services. The services of secretary-typists are now much less needed as executives learn to input material directly on the word processor. For those who feel that typing is undignified for a senior manager, voice-input word processing is just a few years away. Accounting is now superbly performed by appropriate software. Desktop publishing is reducing the demand for traditional typographers. Diagnostic and imaging technology is automating a part of the medical profession.

And the ultimate irony of it all is that computer technology is likely to put computer programmers themselves out of business. When computers were in their infancy, it was almost necessary to be a mathematical genius to use them. Today, it is a question of pointing and clicking with a mouse. A number of intricate languages developed for early computers are now obsolete or museum pieces. As computers get more sophisticated they get, surprisingly, *easier and easier to use* . A state-of-the-art computer of today is user-friendly and requires shorter and shorter learning times. Making full use of it requires no knowledge of programming, any more than eating requires cooking skills or reading requires printing skills.

If informediation were to penetrate the service sector, what would the long-term consequences be? We will be moving, according to Jay Gershuny of Britain and Alvin Toffler of the United States to a *'self-service'* *economy* . We will be demanding fewer services from others and performing more services for ourselves. In fact, the self-service economy is already here, in the form of the informal economy of autonomous individuals less dependent on a 'job' to make a living. The quasi self-sufficient individual is called a 'producer-consumer' or 'prosumer' by Toffler in his *Third Wave* . As 'prosumers' increase, the uncoupling process in the service sector gains momentum. The regular nine-to-five job, working for someone else, may well become a rarity.

Contemporary Trends in
North American Employment.

What does the uncoupling hypothesis mean as far as long-term employment trends are concerned? Does this mean that full employment is no longer possible? Does it mean that we should all become latter-day Luddites and destroy the machines that take our jobs from us?

Before we answer these questions, let us summarize emerging employment trends in North America and most of the OECD countries:

Trend 1: *The rate of unemployment, as measured by official statistics, tends to increase subtly, over time, independent of the business cycle.*

The level of employment has been, traditionally, linked with the business cycle. In pre-informediation times, the unemployment rate would vary with effective demand. The higher the demand, the more jobs created. The lower the demand, the greater the unemployment. Over the last few business cycles, employment growth has not kept pace with the growth of production. Although at times of economic recovery employment does go up, it takes longer and longer to match previous high levels.

In the period 1961-1973, the United States' average unemployment rate was 4.8 percent, Canada's 5.2 percent, and the average for the top seven industrial powers was 2.8 percent. In the next decade, 1974-1984, the United States' rate climbed to 7.2 percent, Canada's to 7.3 percent and the top seven average was 5.5 percent. In fact, one indicator of this long-term increase in unemployment has been the pressure to redefine what we mean by 'full employment'. At one time, 3 percent of the labour force without jobs was considered 'full employment'.

The number of unemployed workers can never be quite zero, because of frictional effects. As people change jobs, at any one moment in time, a certain proportion of the labour force remains temporarily unemployed. However, as that low level becomes more difficult to attain, the notion of 'full employment' is being redefined upwards. Depending on whom you speak to, 6 to 8 percent unemployment is currently considered 'full employment'. Will that definition be revised to 10, 15, 20 percent in the future, as uncoupling proceeds?

<u>Trend 2</u>: *Youth unemployment in Canada and elsewhere tends to be much higher than general unemployment.*

When lay-offs occur, there is a tendency to let go the younger workers. The severity of youth unemployment is a common feature of all the OECD countries. It is usually two to three times higher than the general unemployment.

<u>Trend 3</u>: *Manufacturing is no longer a major job-creating sector.*

In the last decade, manufacturing output increased by 40 percent in the United States, while the number of blue collar workers went down by 5 million. Comparable figures exist for all OECD countries.

<u>Trend 4</u>: *Large firms do not create many new jobs.*

In the period 1984-1986, U.S. firms employing more than 5,000 workers decreased their labour force by a net 342,000 jobs. Those employing 500 to 5,000 workers lost 146,000 jobs. The dominant trend, for both U.S. and Canadian large firms, is downsizing. Very few major firms are substantially increasing their workforce.

<u>Trend 5</u>: *Small and medium-sized firms create most new jobs ...*

For U.S. firms in the 100-500 employee level, there was a net gain of 183,000 jobs in the period 1984-86. At the 20-100 employee level, the net gain was 518,000 and at the very low end of start-ups (0-19 employees) there was the creation of 536,000 net new jobs.

<u>Trend 6</u>: *...but the life expectancy of small and medium-sized firms is only five years.*

What this means is considerable competition in the small and medium-sized firms and a low survival rate. Only ten percent are reputed to survive. Ninety percent fail in this very Darwinistic 'survival of the fittest' market.

<u>Trend 7</u>: *On the whole, the contemporary North American labour market is marked by high turnover and instability.*

Twenty percent of the labour force in North America changes jobs every year (including those who change jobs within the same firm). About half do so voluntarily and the other half involuntarily. The stress levels associated with job changes are high.

<u>Trend 8</u>: *The Service Sector is by far the greatest job producer.*

Of the 19 million jobs created in the United States between 1970 and 1980, 2 million were in primary and secondary occupations and 17 million in services. Fifty-five percent of all jobs are now in the expanded 'information sector' of the economy. Again, the United States figures are fairly representative of most OECD countries.

<u>Trend 9</u>: *Full-time employment is gradually declining.*

In 1984, 38 percent of the North American labour force was employed part-time. Informal jobs, moonlighting and the underground economy are on the rise. The underground economy could account for 20 percent of the U.S. and Canadian GNPs. It is said to be equivalent of about 35 percent of the GNP of Italy. This means that, in that country, one out of three jobs comes from barter, neighbourhood exchanges and self-service.

Trend 10: *Disguised unemployment is probably at least 20 percent.*

Disguised unemployment is not measured by official statistics. Many people who have a job, in the sense of getting a salary every two weeks, have a very low marginal productivity. An OECD study estimated, for instance, that if 20 percent of the white collar labour force stayed home, no one would notice their absence. Overmanning and redundant labour are particularly high in the service sectors and in government employment - but they are difficult to measure. In the public sector, for instance, the productivity of civil servants, given the nature of what they do, is difficult to monitor. We tend to assume that the value of a job to society is what society pays for it by means of a wage. This may, under some circumstances, be true in the private sector where commodities are bought and sold on the open market. It is much more questionable in the public sector, where many jobs can be created artificially by ministerial decree and have little social usefulness. In general, service occupations in both the public and private sectors are not easily amenable to performance tests. As a result, considerable hidden unemployment may exist: the salary is real but the job may be fictitious.

Trend 11: *Informediation is penetrating most fields.*

The number of areas in the process of being penetrated by information technology is expanding daily. At the same time, the list of occupations that, by definition, will never be affected by information technology is getting shorter and shorter.

Trend 12: *Paradoxically, high-tech produces some high-skilled jobs and many more low-skilled ones. User-friendly technology allows for greater penetration and fewer skills.*

Initially, as noted earlier, high technology created a demand for highly skilled jobs. As the technology became more sophisticated the process was reversed. Nowadays, the higher the technology the more it is likely to be useable by mere button-pushing. Although there are notable exceptions to this trend, it is generally true that transparent and easy-to-use technologies have created a demand for lesser-skilled occupations. In some cases, full use of high technology may require zero knowledge of it. This is known as the 'Boeing 747' effect. It is quite possible to enjoy state-of-the-art airline service between continents and know absolutely nothing about flying. It is sufficient to buy a ticket, fasten the seat-belt and enjoy the meal and movie - a handful of crew in the cockpit will guide the flight to its destination!

Some Plausible Scenarios for Future Work.

If the uncoupling of economic growth from human labour is, indeed, a dominant trend, what is the long-term outlook and how can we cope with it? A certain number of scenarios can be identified:

Scenario 1: Recoupling

This scenario supposes that the uncoupling trend, noted above, either turns out to be short-lived or is cancelled by appropriate job-creation policies. It is, in fact, still the conventional wisdom, which links employment levels to the business cycle and not to permanent technological change. If recoupling occurs, if the rates of economic growth and job-creation become almost identical, then that issue will have been removed from the public agenda. But how likely is that to happen?

Technological change tends to fall into two categories: product innovations and process innovations. Product innovations lead to the creation of new products which generate new demand. Other things being equal, product innovations have tended to be job-creating in the past. Process innovations, on the other hand, refer to improvements in the productive process itself, without involving new products. As a rule, process innovations have tended to be job-saving rather than job-creating. In the short run, a new process may create a flurry of new jobs but, in the long run, it tends to replace many more jobs than it creates. This is, in fact, as it should be since freedom from toil has always been the goal of human beings. To create technologies that will complicate and increase the work needed to produce a given object would hardly be regarded as 'progress'. Therefore, process innovations tend to be labour-saving.

Is it possible to arrest technological change, when it is labour saving? The Luddites thought so when they attempted to destroy the steam engines of the first Industrial Revolution. Before them, the Roman emperor, Vespasian, forbade the use of water-wheels in order to preserve jobs and before him, the Egyptian pharaohs built pyramids to keep the slaves employed. If modern day Luddites were to attempt similar job-preserving policies the gains would be short lived.

Of course, by using older technologies, jobs could be created. In fact, the more inefficient the technology the greater the labour needed, other things being equal. In the late fifties, the President of Indonesia, Sukarno, pondered over the choice of two technologies to build a superhighway in his country: tractors or men with spades. His advisors counselled the use of the latter technology because of its much greater job-creation potential. He was on the point of accepting, when another advisor pointed out that if the men were equipped with teaspoons instead of spades, the job-creation effect would be even greater! It is clear that such a *reductio ad absurdum* would lead nowhere. In Montreal, an elaborate econometric study proved that the job creation associated with the 1976 Summer Olympics would be greater, the more money was spent on the construction of the Olympic Stadium. In response, one journalist pointed out that by the same token, if the Olympic Stadium were to be pulled down every fall and rebuilt every spring the job creation would be maximal!

In general, waste may well produce jobs - but at a price. If Canada were to adopt only those technologies that maximize labour use, come what may, with no regard for efficiency, the result would be counter-productive in the end. In trying to save a few jobs in inefficient industries it would run the risk of losing entire industries to foreign competition. Only by hermetically-closing its borders to international competition could it choose the inefficient technology and get away with it. In an open economy this would not be possible.

The recoupling hypothesis pre-supposes that the industries and activities of the future will be very labour-intensive and, furthermore, that the jobs created would be *Canadian* jobs. Even if new activities were indeed labour intensive, it would be by no means sure that the jobs created would be in Canada, as opposed to Southeast Asia which presently has a more disciplined and cheaper labour force.

Scenario 2: Uncoupling Leads To Unemployment.

The 'recoupling' hypothesis appears to rest on heroic assumptions that are not realistic. After informatics, there is a high probability that, in the West at least, a given national product will be producible with a small fraction of the population and the uncoupling trend will continue.

In Scenario 2, the uncoupling process results in considerable unemployment. As owners of businesses become aware that they need fewer workers to maintain high levels of production, they go ahead and reduce their payrolls. The process of downsizing continues and accelerates whenever new technological innovations further diminish the demand for labour by increasing the productivity of existing workers.

It is popularly thought that when a factor of production increases its productivity, more of that factor will automatically be in demand. This is not always true. High productivity may mean less demand for that particular factor of production.

The Nobel Prize winner, Wassily Leontieff, has eloquently illustrated that point by a reference to horses. In his analogy, although horses were being displaced by mechanization in agriculture, the horses' 'labour union' was not worried. Studies it had commissioned demonstrated that the productivity of horses kept going up. As their numbers diminished and total output increased because of mechanization, output per horse naturally also increased. The productivity of the last horse left in agriculture became astronomical and when he, too, was removed the productivity became infinite! The horses' union concludes from this that horses have nothing to worry about. They will get jobs in industry or in services since their productivity is so high ... !

What would it take today to provide full employment for horses? Horses are used nowadays mainly for recreational activities. If enough money were invested in race tracks and horse shows, it could be theoretically possible to employ all horses. However, to do so might cost $200,000 per horse. Unless society wants to achieve the full employment of horses, at any cost, it will shy away from that costly alternative. Full employment of a redundant factor is always possible if one wishes to pay for it, but not plausible if other factors can produce the same products much more cheaply.

The operation of free market forces, under conditions of mechanization plus informediation, tends to increase technological unemployment in the long run. We could, according to this scenario, ultimately arrive at a situation where 20 percent of the labour force would suffice to produce all the goods and services in demand. In the same vein, it is not plausible to imagine a future government efficiently run by 1,000 civil servants and two giant computers. What would happen, in this case, to the 100,000 civil servants presently employed in Canada? They would not be needed and would be sent over to the private sector for employment. But the private sector would not need them either and they would then swell the ranks of the unemployed.

If uncoupling is allowed to become unemployment, then we will be faced with a dual economy: a lucky few working and obtaining high wages and an unlucky majority living off welfare and unemployment checks - an obviously unacceptable situation.

Scenario 3: Uncoupling leads to Exploitation

In Scenario 3, the uncoupling trend also produces a 20/80 split of the population, but with the following difference. Now the lucky majority is made up of the 80 percent who *do not* have to work for a living. The unlucky minority is composed of those who have to keep the economy going. The situation is exploitative and élitist. A leisure class consisting of the majority of the population is fed, clothed and entertained by a minority of workers manning the machines and fixing the robots. The leisure class would then exploit the workers of the new proletariat.

The possibility of Scenario 3 raises the question of where the rights of workers really lie. Since the middle of the nineteenth century, it has become almost self-evident to claim that every person has the right to a job. But there were, and still are, dissenting voices. The nineteenth century socialist, Paul Lafargue, claimed, on the contrary, that the real inalienable right of a human being is to be *free* from work and that the capitalist system traps us all, instead, in a never-ending treadmill of painful labour. The philosopher, Bertrand Russell, once wrote a persuasive essay, appropriately entitled *In Praise of Idleness* . At the height of the Industrial Revolution in Britain, the famous epitaph of the charwoman was that, in her grave, she would be envied by all because, at last, she would "do nothing and nothing for all of eternity." In fact, it may well be argued that the modern emphasis on the 'right to work' seems to be a culturally-conditioned trait not found in all human cultures and possibly connected, in the West, to the Protestant ethic. Some other cultures may, instead, emphasize the right to be free from work.

Scenario 4: Uncoupling Leads To "Athens without the Slaves".

The fourth scenario introduces the possibility of a leisure society where the uncoupling trend is harnessed and produces positive results for all. We like to call it "Athens without the Slaves" because of its similarity with some aspects of Plato's Republic. In fifth-century Athens, (the source of inspiration for Plato's Republic), an intellectually productive leisure class of poets, philosophers and artists thrived but was supported in its endeavours by the toils of an army of slaves. The 'citizens' did the philosophizing and the poetry while the 'non-citizens' worked hard to keep the economy going. Athens *with* the slaves was, therefore, an imperfect society: a golden age in some senses, but a dark age as far as equality of opportunity was concerned.

Athens *without* the slaves is, theoretically, possible now due to the information revolution. The robots can be entrusted with major production chores and the 'citizens', in this case the whole of society and not just a fraction of it, would be able to enjoy and make good use of their newfound leisure. The mechanism for such a transition is clear. Everyone 'works' progressively-less while continuing to increase his or her personal income. The productivity benefits of automation are shared by all, not just by a lucky majority or minority. The method of dissemination of these benefits is the progressive *time - freedom* or *leisure,* if you will, bestowed on the population.

At first glance, this scenario may appear hopelessly futuristic. On closer analysis, it will be discovered that the progressive liberation of human time from the constraints of work has, in fact, been the historical scenario of the last two hundred years.

When mechanization started to transform the production function something very basic occurred: *the quantum of work needed to produce a given output was reduced.* This 'quantum of work' is best measured not in 'jobs' but in time - hours, days or, more suitably, person-years.

A century ago, around 1870, the annual quantum of work in North America was 3,000 hours per employed person. Today, the work-year is about 1,500 hours, some of which are 'soft' hours, (coffee and lunch breaks, or sitting around time). At 1,500 hours, we have a visible unemployment rate that hovers around the 10 percent mark and a hidden unemployment rate of perhaps another 20 percent. Therefore, for all intents and purposes, we produce what is needed to satisfy our current needs with much less than 1,500 hours. What would happen if we were to return to a 3,000-hour year? Unless there were to be a doubling of demand and technology remained unchanged, the increase in the work-year would result in more unemployment. Conversely, if we were to reduce the work year say to 1,000 hours, then unemployment could be diminished.

In other words, for a given level of technology, there is a corresponding quantum of work which would create full employment . Econometric studies would show us what that quantum is at any point in time. Instead of taking the redundant hours in the form of unemployment (some people working 1,500 hours and others none at all) we would take them in the form of a reduction of work time. Everybody would be working less.

This is where we come to a fork in the road: working less with less pay or working less with equal or more pay? Naturally, it is in the employer's interest to minimize labour costs. Ideally, the worker should work more and be paid less, not vice-versa. This was always true and should not be surprising. However, the experience of the last two hundred years has shown that employers, sometimes prodded by legislation, sometimes on their own, have agreed to share the benefits of mechanization with their workers. If this were not so, we would still have a 3,000-hour work-year. We do not. Instead, workers today work half of what they used to and earn considerably more. What has happened is that, in an expanding economy, the employers have shared the growing 'pie' with the workers.

The coming of informediation has accelerated the reduction of the quantum of work needed for full production. As a result, matters are coming to a head: either the benefits of uncoupling will be shared, or a dual economy will be created where one part of the population works and the other does not.

Let us return to the example of mechanization in agriculture, as cited by Wassily Leontieff. In that particular case, two factors of production were made redundant: horses and the sons of farmers who were now no longer needed. The horses were fired but the sons of farmers shared in the profits of the household. In the same sense, modern companies can choose to treat their workers as 'horses' or as 'sons and daughters'. In the North American tradition, labour is seen primarily as an expense and lay-offs are natural if this will increase profits. The 'horse' metaphor prevails. In the Japanese tradition, at least as far as large firms are concerned, workers are seen as 'sons and daughters' and are kept on the payroll, in spite of automation. In fact, the permanent employment policy of large Japanese firms tends to allay the fears of workers and creates a 'win/win' situation which favours labour/management co-operation.

One of the major marvels of the Japanese industrial system is that it has succeeded in maintaining 'feudal' values in advanced capitalism. One of the characteristics

of the feudal system was the permanent employment of
agricultural workers (as exploited serfs, to be sure) in the
production system. The wages were low but there was job-
security and permanent loyalty to the lord of the land. In
the Japanese industrial system, the large firms are like
feudal units, granting job security to their members and
expecting loyalty. The loyalty is nurtured by company
songs, uniforms, and corporate culture. The job security -
unlike in the old feudal system - is not necessarily
exploitative, since contemporary Japanese workers have a
reasonably high standard of living.

To return to the 'working less, earning more'
scenario that is the essence of the "Athens without the
Slaves" model of society: it is eminently possible if an
agreement in principle is made to share the benefits of
technology among all. It would help, of course, if the trend
were worldwide. Obviously, if in some countries workers
are fired in favour of more efficient and cheaper robots and
in other countries they are kept on to share in the profits,
the latter countries will be handicapped and be less
competitive. The present world-wide drive is to encourage
downsizing and lower employment levels. *This trend can
only be reversed if everybody agrees to do so.*

An additional element must be introduced here: the
changing nature of what we call 'work' and 'working'. As
the weight of the economy has shifted from agricultural
and manufactured products to services, the nature of what
we call 'products' has become much less tangible. The
proliferation of consultants for virtually everything, the
surge of the entertainment business and the multiplier
effects of media have profoundly modified our pre-
conceived ideas about what human labour is.   When
Frank Sinatra gets $50,000 for singing "God Bless

America" on a Fourth of July celebration, or Michael Tyson gets $10 million, in one minute, for knocking out his heavyweight opponent in a title bout what, in fact, have they produced? Essentially illusions, perceptions, feelings. "We are such stuff as dreams are made on," said Shakespeare, "and our little life is rounded with a sleep."

A particularly difficult distinction to make nowadays is between the traditional concepts of 'work' and 'leisure'. Conventional wisdom tends to claim that 'work' is when one is productive and getting paid and 'leisure' is when one is not. This distinction is weakening, since not all paid work is 'productive', as we have seen earlier, and not all unpaid activities 'unproductive'.

It is a matter of perceptions. Consider the case of the two neighbours. The first is a professional tennis player who practices his tennis from nine to five and relaxes after that by playing the piano. The second is a professional pianist. He practices his scales from nine to five and plays tennis to relax. There is nothing intrinsic in either occupation which pre-determines its status as 'work' or 'leisure'. It is principally a matter of perception.

In exploring the remaining distinctions between work and leisure, some have claimed that 'work' is 'painful', while 'leisure' is 'pleasurable'. That distinction is also increasingly suspect. Quite apart from advocating a sort of 'masochistic' theory of remuneration (if you are not suffering, you should not get paid), it goes against the productivity theory. The most creative and productive individuals, the geniuses of our time in every field, make no such distinction between work and leisure. They love their work and would probably do it for nothing. Top executives, top artists, top intellectuals, in effect, uncouple their work from the remuneration they get. One would not expect to see a great artist decide to be more creative as the pay goes up. The fee is a by-product of a highly pleasurable activity which, coincidentally, is also highly lucrative. In fact, a possible indicator of a happy person is precisely one for whom the distinction between work and leisure has become blurred.

The Need for Tripartite Co-operation.

On the Canadian scene, the future of labour after informatics must be viewed in the context of a necessary tripartite co-operation between labour, management and government. In the present situation, the relations are clearly adversarial. Canada's strike record rivals Italy's, where even the Supreme Court once went on strike. However, the Italian strike experience is more akin to a cultural ritual of going through the moves than a substantive problem. Informal dealings and 'under-the-table' agreements usually end the strikes before the antagonists 'reach for each other's jugular'. In Canada, too often the 'lunge for the jugular' is automatic, with deleterious results as far as image, productivity and competitiveness are concerned.

In marked contrast to Canada's industrial relations experience is that of Austria. During the year 1980, Austria lost exactly *six man-hours* as a result of strikes. Canada, with a population three times that of Austria, racked up *eight million man-days* lost. Japan used to be strike-ridden in the sixties and early seventies (three million days lost in 1970 versus six million lost in Canada in the same year), but has become more consensual and less strike-prone. In both Japan and Austria, tripartite joint planning is the rule of the day and the proactive stance of the three groups smooths out difficulties *before* they

occur. If Canada is going to compete successfully, it will
have to adopt similar strategies.

    The existing institutions for co-operative joint
planning are not successful since they tend to transpose
within them Canada's adversarial ethic. The Economic
Council of Canada is frequently the arena, not for tripartite
co-operation, but rather for a tripartite 'free-for-all' where
each sector vehemently defends its interests. The long-
term solution for managing the labour/management
interface is to emphasize the 'win/win' aspects of co-
operation and the 'lose/lose' aspects of conflict. Workers
must be given the security and assurance of profit-sharing
and of time-freeing, permanent employment schemes. As
well, the entire unemployment insurance system must be
revamped - in the light of the new realities and not by
pretending that unemployment is only related to business
cycles, as in the paradigm still dominant among politicians
and their advisors. There is an urgent need for innovative
thinking - and rethinking - in this area.

Chapter 8

CONSENSUS ECONOMIES : PROS AND CONS

We have argued that a network of adversary systems governs Canada today, with government rivalling government, public sector clashing with private sector and labour wrangling with managment. There is a fourth major adversary system in play, one that comes out of the functioning of the private sector itself.

Competition is, of course, the basis of the market system and has considerable virtues. A system based on competition is extremely dynamic and productive, and even its critics, from Karl Marx on, have recognized its creative and growth potential. What must be explored is where precisely the advantages of the market system lie and who benefits from them. Is the Canadian small firm vs. small firm struggle the best national economic strategy in a complex and dangerous world?

In Joseph Schumpeter's terms, competition trims the fat from the economy by eliminating marginal firms. Only the best survive and this process becomes a sort of economic 'eugenics' - a selective breeding of high performers. In a pure market system, the winners take all. In a mixed market system, the winners are not allowed to take all. Instead, they are kept in check by taxes and other forms of public regulation. Our existing system allows winners to take some of the spoils and the losers obtain some compensation through tax breaks. It is a hybrid system and represents a compromise. But how far is it a good compromise?

To answer this question, we must bear in mind that there are, in today's contemporary world, basically three distinct models of economic organization. The first is the *individually-competitive mode* that is prevalent in a number of countries, such as the United States, Canada, Britain, and Australia. It pits firm against firm and ultimately individual against individual. Competition is maximized. The second model favours *central planning and command economies.* Here, a strong central government takes upon itself the task of pre-planning, regulating and leading the national economy towards fixed goals. The command economy, typically, uses five-year plans which are imperative and binding. The most well-known examples come from the Soviet Union and Eastern Europe. The third model, of comparatively recent vintage, is the *group-competitive mode.* It is similar to the individually-competitive model in that it recognizes and attempts to use the virtues of competition to bring about excellence. But it is also similar to the command economy model in that it gives the state an important role, beyond running the army and cleaning the streets. Its focus is on group competition. National clusters of firms, conglomerates so to speak, are sent out to compete on the world stage. The paragon of that particular model is, of course, Japan - in some sense, the most capitalistic and, in other senses, the most socialistic of the major economies. But Japan is not alone. The group-competitive mode is also favoured in France, Germany, Austria and the 'Mini-Dragons' of Southeast Asia: Taiwan, Hong-Kong, Singapore and South Korea.

A major question for Canada and other Western countries is whether the individually-competitive adversarial model, which we cherish, is a winning combination in today's complex world. Before we attempt to answer this question let us deepen our understanding of the three models.

Individual Competitive Economies.

The best example of the individually-competitive model is the United States. The American political and economic systems are both imbued with this philosophy. At the political level, the system is based on the doctrine of separation of powers. As interpreted in the United States, separation of powers should be read as 'conflict of powers'. Although there are weaker adversarial relations between levels of government in the United States than there are in Canada, the competition between branches of government is very high. The executive branch proposes but the legislative branch, fully independent and autonomous, may challenge, modify and refuse initiatives emanating from the executive branch and substitute its own. The judicial branch has no initiative but has immense veto power, since it can fully block initiatives of either of the other two branches by declaring them unconstitutional. The nature of the system can be summed up in two words: *watchdog democracy.* The power of any one unit in the system must be checked and balanced by a watchdog group in another area.

The economic system emulates the political. The corporate units, of which it is composed, have chief executive officers (CEOs), who often report to another head of the company, the chairman of the board. In some cases, the two functions are merged, but in the pure system the executive officer is controlled by the board, which acts as the 'congress' of the corporation. In France, there is usually one head of the firm, the 'PDG' (president-directeur-general), while in the American system the responsibilities are divided. Within each corporation, the different sub-units compete for funds, and often see themselves as independent units within the corporate whole. Thus, it is quite possible for "Division A" to try to put "Division B" out of business. In addition, individual competition prevails, where each executive tries to advance at the expense of the others. The intra-firm competitive mode is sometimes much fiercer than the inter-firm, as senior managers compete for the top positions.

The American stress on individual competition naturally leads to anti-trust laws. The U.S. government views, with great suspicion, any attempt by two or more companies to collaborate in any fashion. This is in marked contrast to the group-competitive countries who encourage their national corporations to work together. In the U.S. system, everyone must compete on an individual basis, come what may. There are unmistakeable signs that this attitude hampers U.S. competitiveness, in particular with respect to Japan, and especially in the area of major technological innovations. The United States has found it necessary to build consortia of firms to meet the Japanese challenge. Individual competition, in this field, is doomed.

The individually-competitive philosophy also manifests itself in the military field. Inter-service rivalry is proverbial in America. The Joint Chiefs of Staff constitute a model adversary system, with the Chairman being just the first among equals. Examples of the negative effects of this rivalry abound. First, expenditure on weapons systems is consistently wasteful as the three services compete and duplicate each others' initiatives. The long debate over the effectiveness of the MX missile, for instance, saw the Air Force on opposition to the other services. Even if, say, a submarine-based defensive system would, objectively, be judged to be better, the nature of the adversarial system forces each service to push its own system, come what may. As a result, many dollars are thrown at the defence problem with little additional security achieved.

The so-called Rapid Deployment Force, supposedly an inter-service joint effort under adversarial rules, has been derided as being "neither rapid, nor deployed, nor particularly forceful". In the aborted commando raid, in Iran in 1980, the full extent of the underlying adversarial system was exposed. First, the system of checks and balances forced the then-president of the United States, Jimmy Carter, to ask overt permission from Congress for conduct which was obviously a covert operation. Secondly, in this and other instances, the American press has shown its inability or unwillingness to keep a national secret. If a story can make news, then the national interest is set aside. Finally, at the operational level, when the raid turned sour because of miscues, everyone accused everyone else. Marine helicopters were abandoned on-site by Air Force personnel under the pretext that "they were not their responsibility".

The United Kingdom is another advanced example of a structural adversary system, but with one important difference: self-restraint. British parliamentary democracy is based on a version of separation of powers that expresses itself by the explicit duty of the party not in government to systematically 'oppose'. The 'Official Opposition', as it is known in both Britain and Canada, has as its raison d'être the perpetual critique of government initiatives, as a matter of course, whether they be objectively good or bad. This role must be played to the hilt The party out of power is known not only as the 'Opposition' but also as the 'Queen's

Most Loyal Opposition', implying that systematically to oppose is not to be disloyal. This opposition idea also spills over to the judicial system. Barristers, solicitors and attorneys, for the various parties, are supposed to give priority to their client's interest, not the objective truth. Somehow, it is assumed that the truth will emerge from this dialectical conflict, completely ignoring the possibility that a skilled lawyer may win a bad cause and an unskilled one lose a good cause. This adversarial judicial system is in marked contrast with those of some other countries, where the search for the truth is the primary responsibility of *all parties* and the defence of the client a secondary responsibility.

The emphasis on individual interest in the United States, Britain and Canada increases the probability of lawsuits and creates a strong demand for the services of the legal profession: these three countries have, on average, ten times as many lawyers per capita as Japan. In the United States, in particular, one can threaten to sue for practically anything.

The distinguishing feature of the British adversary system has been its historic adherence to the "Marquess of Queensbury rules", where conflict is limited according to unwritten conventions. As an example of this restraint, we have but to look at British constitutional law. As is well known, Britain has no Constitution. A number of Acts of Parliament, such as Magna Carta, have special psychological status. On paper, however, the Queen is sovereign and the British Parliament may, if it so desires, legislate itself into a dictatorship. There is nothing to prevent a given Parliament from repealing all the laws of previous Parliaments. In other countries this could be a formula for chaos. In Britain, the reliance on convention and gentlemen's agreements has withstood the test of time and there has been no constitutional crisis, to speak of, since the Roundheads opposed the Cavaliers in the seventeenth century. Britain does not need an explicit Meech Lake type of constitution. It has functioned well by implicit understandings. The mistake, of course, is to assume that a British-type system would automatically work in other cultures.

On the economic front, however, Britain's adversarial system has not succeeded so well. Since the Second World War, it has sapped the strength and vitality of the British economy. The continual labour versus management conflict has led to the infamous "British disease" of the seventies: loss of competitiveness by an economy where all parties want to get a larger share of the 'pie' - even if this means that the 'pie' will get absolutely smaller. The success of British constitutional law has definitely not been matched by equivalent economic successes. All told, although the economic fortunes of Britain appear much better at the end of the eighties than at the beginning of the decade, it is still too early to tell whether a long-term recovery is in the offing. At the time of writing, Britain remains one of the poorest countries of Europe, after having been by far the richest and having led the world into the era of industrialization.

Two pathological extremes in the individual-competitive model are Argentina and Lebanon. In Argentina's case, the country never realized its immense potential because of the tendency of its major players constantly to cancel-out each other. Five major groupings have, in the last hundred years, vied for power: the landowners, the businessmen, the workers, the clergy and the armed forces. The latter have been beset by even greater inter-service rivalries than their U.S. counterparts. As a result, the Argentinean economy has never achieved the critical minimum threshold necessary for successful world-class competition.

But the Argentinean experience pales before the all-time champion of the adversarial mode, Lebanon. The last two decades have been very painful indeed for a country so well-endowed with dynamic human resources and world-class entrepreneurs. Adversarial groups have multiplied freely, to the point that it is impossible to draw battle lines. Not only do Christians fight Moslems and both fight Palestinians and all three fight Israelis, but each of these groupings have serious internal fights. The Christians fight each other, and the Moslems kill each other with abandon. Even radical sub-groups, such as the Shiites sprout sub-sub groups almost *ad infinitum* , so that *Hezbollah* fights *Amal* and so on and so forth. The general cancellation of effort that results from these civil wars is testimony to the bankruptcy of the adversarial philosophy.

Command Economies (Centrally Planned)

An alternative to the individually competitive economies is the *command economy.* In that model, a central organization, typically but not always a government, directs the economy and organizes its operation. Such an economy can be driven either from the Left by a socialist-communist government, or from the extreme Right by a totalitarian fascist-type regime. How have such economies fared?

The most important case is, of course, that of the Soviet Union. In the fifty years from the Bolshevik Revolution to the Brezhnev era, it is obvious that Russia made enormous strides. From a backward, agricultural nation it became a major superpower, both militarily and economically. However, it is not clear whether there is a sufficient cause-effect relationship to justify attributing that progress to the centrally-planned economic model. Evidence suggests that the Russian industrial take-off had taken place at least two decades before the Bolshevik Revolution - which implies that the ensuing economic progress would have occurred anyway. Whatever the judgement on the period, from 1917 to 1967, the more recent performance of the U.S.S.R. economy has not been brilliant. The efforts of Mikhail Gorbachev, in the late eighties, to restructure the Russian economic system (*perestroika*) and open it to the world (*glasnost*) is telling evidence of failure. Similar failures have been noted in other Eastern European countries (and which have even brought down the government), particularly Poland and Romania, who have not realized what they had set out to do via the command economy mode.

The experience of China is also interesting. After the Cultural Revolution experiment and extreme Maoism, once 'Red' China is becoming more and more 'Blue'. The projected re-annexation of Hong-Kong, at the end of the century, presages what, in effect, may turn out to be a counter-annexation. The Hong-Kong system may be extended to the whole of China, rather than vice-versa. The events of spring 1989, and the repressive measures of the hard-liners against the Beijing students, may delay the agenda by a number of years or decades. However, what is clear is that the command economy, Chinese style, has not proven itself as a major development instrument.

On the whole, command economies have not shown that they can compete effectively and achieve world-class successes in the economic arena, although they have produced muscle-bound military superpowers and Olympic champions.

Group Competitive Economies.

Lying somewhere between the individually competitive and command models is the third model, which we have called "group-competitive". Its essential features are basically two. First and foremost, the *national players work as a team* and collaborate rather than compete. Competition is relegated to the international scene. Second, *the national government acts as 'maestro', 'co-ordinator' or 'coach' of that team.* It does not attempt to replace the team or be an active player itself, like in the command economy model, nor does it completely eclipse itself from the game, as is the case in the pure model of individual competition. It gives guidance, advice and support, but not much more.

If the United States is the model of the individually competitive economy and the Soviet Union the model of central planning, Japan is the champion of group-competitiveness.

The Japanese system is rooted in the traditional culture and values of the country, but it is important to realize that Japan was not always a consensus, group-competitive economy. Before the Meiji Restoration of the 1860s, Japan was an adversarial society kept in check by a ruthless Shogun. The recourse to a Shogun succeeded many centuries of adversarial in-fighting and tribal warfare. The Shogun was the pacifier. He was the military chief ruling the country for the Emperor. After the Meiji restoration, the authority of the Emperor was restored and made more direct and the seeds of the contemporary emphasis on consensus began to take root.

The most important elements of the Japanese consensus may be summarized as follows. First, the outlook is long-term and not short-term. Development projects are evaluated in decades, not years. "Short-term pain for long-term gain" is accepted as a basic strategic principle. Second, the national interest is considered supreme and individual interests are subordinate to it. The national interest is symbolically-centred around the person of the Emperor, who maintains a quasi-divine image for his people. Third, the business sector is organized, not in small competing units, but in large conglomerates, highly diversified and able to re-deploy resources, capital and labour according to the dictates and opportunities of the market. Fourth, organized labour is part of the consensus and not excluded from it. It participates in joint planning exercises. Fifth, the banking community is an active player in the economy. It is not just a lender of funds - it assumes part of the risk. In that sense, it does not view its clients in an adversarial capacity but instead sees them as allies. Japanese bankers are patient and will tolerate very long payback times. This allows the system to work with long-range targets, rather than attempt to maximize quarterly profits. Sixth, the government acts as a provider of information, as a go-between, as a coach and as an advisor, but rarely as an active player. The weight of the Japanese public sector in the economy is, surprisingly, lighter than that of the American government in the United States. Finally, Japan uses internal competition between Japanese firms in the same way that national Olympic committees use qualifying heats to try out athletes before choosing the final team. The internal competition is part of the training process but, once that is complete, the firms are sent out to conquer foreign markets in co-ordinated fashion. This means that there is considerable explicit and implicit co-operation between Japanese firms abroad. They share a common information base, allocate marketing targets and conduct joint research and development.

The Japanese system may be loved or hated, admired or despised, but it is very difficult to claim that, so far, it has failed. On the contrary, it has allowed that country, which was, in 1945, at about the same economic level as Sri Lanka, to forge ahead and become number one in major economic areas. In essence, the Japanese economy is centrally co-ordinated by a permanent quartet of four major players: MITI (The Ministry of International Trade and Industry), the major banks, the conglomerates or *Zaibatsus* and the trading companies or *Sogososha*.

Is the Japanese experience exportable? Can we learn from it? Or is it inextricably linked to Japanese culture? Are there other Japans, actual or potential? The Japanese are the first to try to convince the West that their experience is a unique case and cannot be emulated elsewhere. Since much of the competitive advantage of Japan is based on the hope of non-imitation, discouraging emulation is natural.

Yet, once abstracted from its particular cultural artifacts, the Japanese consensus economy is *but one prototype among many* of the emerging 'third way'. At least four Asian countries are following in Japan's footsteps and at least another four European countries have versions of consensus economies. The four Asian 'neo-Japans' are South Korea, Taiwan, Singapore and now China. All four have similar Confucian ethic values which favour group-competition, as opposed to the individual-competition bias of the Protestant ethic. All four have disciplined labour forces, very clear objectives and a

national will to make it happen. From Canada's point of
view, however, Asian examples are less convincing than
Western ones. This is why we will now focus on some of
the European cousins of the Japanese consensus model.

Perhaps the country that is intellectually closest to
Japan, in Western Europe, is France. This is not because
France has absorbed Japanese ideas more than others. It is,
more significantly, because the French have arrived at
conclusions very similar to those of the Japanese - not this
year, not last, but a full three centuries ago. As was
indicated earlier, France was the first country to develop a
coherent theory of the group-competitive economy under
the name of "Colbertism". The brainchild of Jean-Baptiste
Colbert, the Intendant of Louis XIV, Colbertism has
dominated, in implicit or explicit form, most French
governments from Louis XIV to De Gaulle, Pompidou,
Giscard d'Estaing and Mitterand. French economic policy
has, in general, been above party politics and has reflected
some degree of consensus as to objectives, although
individual political parties have selected different means to
attain those ends.

A key element of Colbertism, that both the French
and Japanese systems share, is the subordination of
economic policy to national purpose. In Colbert's time, the
national purpose was the *agrandissement* of France and
the increase in power of Louis XIV. As a means to that
end, Colbert believed in maximizing exports and
accumulating gold and silver. The Japanese also believe in
maximizing exports and accumulating not only cash
balances but also investment abroad. Colbert explicitly
referred to French companies as 'armies'. The *Compagnie
des Indes Orientales* and the *Compagnie des Habitants*
were meant to establish footholds in the colonies and

expand them to serve the mother country. In today's
France, a number of nationalized firms, the equivalent of
our Crown corporations, are major players in world
industry and world finance. French nationalized banks
figure prominently among the top ten financial institutions
in the world. Like the Japanese companies, the French
multinationals act in the general interest of the nation
although, of course, the nationalized firms do this more
explicitly than the others.

France's strong point as a group-competitive
economy is its remarkable public sector/private sector
collaboration. The French government provides
information, seed funds and a general 'indicative' plan, for
the economy as a whole, pointing to the road ahead. This
plan is not imperative or binding as in a command
economy, but more 'suggestive'. It is accompanied by a
series of 'carrots and sticks' - incentives and disincentives
- to motivate the private sector to come onside. French
indicative planning is less explicit now than it was in the
post-war years, but it continues in some form or other and
provides the basis for a successful public/private interface.
A feature of this collaboration that is similar to Japan's is
the notion of 'national champions'. The French
government encourages competition between firms to
select a national champion. Once this champion is
identified, other firms are encouraged to merge or form
strategic networks with the national champion. As a result,
France is able to enter heavyweight contenders in the
international 'economic olympics' and not just small
individual firms.

France's weakness in the group-competitive context
is its adversarial labour/management interface. Perhaps
not as intense as Italy's or Britain's, that particular

adversary system remains strong and acts as a significant brake for French enterprise.

Another weakness of the French system is its inability to implement fully a plan, even if that plan is completely coherent. In 1978-79, the French government ordered and obtained a comprehensive study on the potential of information technology for society as a whole, including its effects on competitiveness. The study was authored by two senior civil servants and was known as the Nora-Minc Report (Simon Nora and Alain Minc, *L'informatisation de la société*). It was, at the time, a state-of-the-art statement and had no equal elsewhere for comprehensiveness and insight. Even the Japanese studies, in comparison, appeared confused on many issues. Yet, in terms of implementation, this remarkable report has been a failure. It has not succeeded in propelling France to the excellence it targeted in the fields of telematics, although it did make that country into a major contender.

The time-lag, between the conceptualization of a problem and the actualization of policies to resolve it, is an acknowledged weakness of the overly-Cartesian French system. The plan is perfect but its actualization often woefully defective. The Japanese, on the other hand, are less conceptual and less immersed in Aristotelian logic; they are, however, more pragmatic. They are much faster off the mark and race to the finish line while other countries are still pondering options and alternatives.

Germany is another group-competitive economy. Its group-competitive stance stems from an intense nationalism which has driven the country from the time of German unification in 1871. The loss of two world wars and an enforced partition have not deterred this country from dominating the European economy. West Germany is the powerhouse of Western Europe and East Germany the economic and technological leader of Eastern Europe. The sense of national purpose has given rise to a collaborative, rather than an adversarial, mode between labour and management and a concerted action between the private and public sectors. In addition, although the federal states of Germany enjoy substantial autonomy, they place that autonomy in context and would not think of competing against each other on the international scene like Canadian provinces do.

Another interesting group-competitive economy is Switzerland. Organized as a decentralized confederation, the Swiss cantons are mini-states; in addition, like Canada, Switzerland is multi-ethnic and multicultural. However, what induces the Swiss to work together, rather than against each other, is a common tradition of excellence and achievement. Rather than interfere with a winning combination, the Swiss balance opposing interests, allow regional autonomy and encourage the private sector to form whatever strategic alliances are necessary to achieve excellence on the world stage.

Sweden is another interesting prototype. A backward agricultural country a century ago, on the verge of bankruptcy and ecological disaster, the Swedes turned their economy around, stayed out of European wars and forged a unique private/public collaboration scheme which has no equivalent elsewhere. Interlocking directorates of private firms with government bodies have allowed a handful of individuals to impart a 'Team-Sweden' approach to problems of international competition, so far with excellent results. Sweden's standard of living is among the highest in the world and its social programmes provide safety nets for the entire population.

Finally, Austria must be mentioned, once again, as a success story. During the 1970s, when the rest of the Western world was wallowing in stagflation - strong inflation coupled with massive unemployment - the Austrian economy emerged unscathed. Its unemployment rate was 2 percent and its inflation rate 3 percent. It steadily introduced automation into its productive process and, therefore, remained very competitive. As the basis for the Austrian system was a well thought-out, well-executed tripartite team approach, involving industry, labour and government.

The Place of Competition in Strategic Theory.

The evidence of the last two decades clearly points to the success of the group-competitive economies and the comparative failure of both the individual-competitive and the command economies. Why is this so and how does this shed new light on the place of competition in strategic theory?

By way of introduction to this question, let me recount an event which I experienced in Egypt a few years ago. Visiting the Pyramids with some friends I noticed an Egyptian 'dragoman' or semi-official guide talk to a Japanese tourist. The Egyptian, schooled in the arts of vending, was selling to the Japanese all sorts of worthless goodies, fake bibelots, post cards, souvenirs, and tickets to night-clubs. The Japanese tourist, with his Hawaiian shirt and perennial camera slung across his neck, appeared defenceless - the perfect mark in a classic sting. Seeing this obvious imbalance, I wondered how it was that Egypt was not doing as well as Japan, since there were very many enterprising 'dragomen' in the country. The answer came in a flash. In a one-on-one, I would choose the wily

Egyptian over the naïve, smiling Japanese. But multiply each side by a hundred, a thousand or a million and it would be no contest. A million Egyptians would cancel each other out and live in poverty, while a million Japanese would buy the Pyramids, irrigate the desert and industrialize the country in a short period of time. The difference is the ability or inability to *work in teams* . The Japanese have been conditioned, by history and culture, to work in teams. The Egyptians have not. Temperamentally individualistic, like the Lebanese, they have, like many other cultures, greater difficulty in forming teams than the Japanese.

In similar fashion, one cannot but marvel at the ingenuity and spirit of enterprise of Mexican peddlers on the beaches of Acapulco or the Senegalese beggars in Dakar. Their sense of pre-sale service and marketing skills are admirable. The eleven-year-old Mexican peddler is a study in entrepreneurship. He begins by offering everything for one peso. Then, by elaborate stories he tells you that unless he sells so many souvenirs his parents are going to beat him. The Senegalese street peddler is even more ingenuous. Eight years old and charming, he will begin by offering you a souvenir as a free gift, to "thank Canada for what it has done for his brother who has emigrated there". The offer of the gift is followed by an irresistible sales pitch that results, in most cases, in great success. The techniques used rival those of Harvard Business School but, unfortunately, when large numbers are involved they tend to peter out. The individual competitive advantage completely disappears when a larger network is involved.

The ability to function in large numbers and work in teams has now become a survival skill in the complex international economy. This fact has nothing to do with ideology. It has to do with the 'nature of the game'. Singles tennis opposes two individuals in a classic one-on-one duel. Doubles tennis requires co-ordination between the partners on the same team.

Hockey, soccer and football are fundamentally different from singles tennis, because success or failure depends almost entirely on group cohesion. Our cocky National Hockey League and our successive Team Canadas have had rude awakenings in their meetings with Soviet teams over the last fifteen years. The NHL superstars, arguably better one-on-one, have been repeatedly humiliated by lesser teams with much greater cohesion.

A system that maximizes competition *between players on the same team* may, inadvertently, weaken rather than strengthen that team. Assume, for instance, a hockey system which only gives points to goals and not to assists. In such a system no one will ever pass to a teammate. Each player will try to score on his own, with the probable result that very few goals will be scored. Assume, on the other hand, an opposite system which credits goals not to the individual who puts the puck in the net but to the entire three-man line. In that system, the playmaker gets as much credit as the scorer. Other things being equal, that system will produce more goals than the individualistic one.

The realization that hockey is a team game has been slow to sink in, even for the country that invented the game. It has taken more than a decade for Canadian hockey teams to learn that lesson and work on group cohesion. An interesting indicator of the team character of hockey has been that established Canadian clubs, with players who work together year-long, have performed better against the Soviets than all-star teams who have only had two or three practices before the big game.

The metaphor of hockey is an apt one to describe how the international economy has changed. Everywhere, the name of the game is networking, partnering, mergers, acquisitions and strategic alliances. The lone rangers are usually eliminated very early in the game. The contestants who make it to the playoffs are linked firms.

The decade-old rash of mergers and acquisitions in North America illustrates that point. So does, for that matter, the management strategy of 'partnering' which is the implementation of joint ventures in specific areas. In the field of technology strategy, for instance, university/industry co-operation and government/business joint ventures can produce excellent results. In addition, the penetration of foreign markets is often best achieved not by 'parachuting products out of the blue' but by establishing a strategic alliance between the exporter and a local firm.

Are there, then, no benefits associated with good old-fashioned competition? Of course there are, but they must be placed in proper context. In the first place, a distinction must be made between *the benefits of competition which accrue to the competitors and those that accrue to others* . Competition benefits the competitors themselves in two cases. The first occurs when, through competition with firm "B", firm "A" learns to become more efficient and a better competitor generally. "B" then acts as a sparring partner for "A". "A" then goes ahead and meets other competitors more successfully. This is the *training* benefit. A second benefit is obtained if the successful firm is allowed to reap the *spoils of victory*

- that is if it wins and becomes a monopolist. If firm "A" can, through competition, eliminate firm "B" to corner the market, then the possibility of winning makes competition worthwhile for firm "A". If there is no real possibility of winning, then competition is much less attractive to the competitors themselves. It is unclear whether it is, in fact, possible fully to 'win', according to the rules of our economic system. Monopolies are frowned upon, excessive profits looked at with suspicion and often taxed away. Winning, then, becomes quite relative in the national context.

A key condition for competition to be beneficial to the competitors themselves is that the game played be of the zero-sum variety. A zero-sum game is one where whatever one wins the others lose. The size of the 'pie' is fixed. The game is a 'win/lose' activity. If the game is a 'win/win' (positive sum) or 'lose/lose' (negative sum), competition is not in the interest of the competitors. In 'win/win' situations, competitors tend to co-operate, not because they like each other, but because they realize that it is in their interest to do so. For example, oligopolists tend to want to collude and fix prices They correctly believe that by concerting their efforts they can each make more money. The game is 'win/win' for them. This is why anti-trust and anti-combines legislation tries to prevent such collusion. Similarly, in the 'lose/lose' games, the competitors have a vested interest in co-operating. A price war is the prime example of a 'lose/lose' situation. Left to their rational selves, sellers attempt to avoid price wars, if at all possible, and co-operate to fix prices.

When the game is not zero-sum with the possibility of a clear winner, and there is no meaningful training effect, *competition is worthless* for the competitors and all its benefits go to third parties. When the third parties are consumers or society as a whole, competition is then deemed to be socially good. A price war is ideal for the buyer, who can then sit back and watch sellers improve their offerings. Ultimately, from a third party viewpoint, there is an interest in a 'gladiator' economy, where a number of industrial gladiators tear each other to pieces to please the consuming public. But from the point of view of the gladiators, themselves, this option is not particularly desirable.

What, then, should be the proper locus of competitive activity? Should we maximize internal competition in order to get our local gladiators to produce more and better products? Or should we select national champions to compete with those of other countries in the international arena? The answers to these questions depend on the importance one attaches to the nation-state. Those who believe the nation-state is dead would prefer the first formula which, in effect, gives free reign to world multinationals regardless of national origin. In such a system, national development policies, industrial strategies and group-competitiveness are meaningless. Free competition should prevail and we, as consumers, should reap the benefits of lower prices and better products, come what may. If this means favouring foreign enterprises over our own, so be it.

For those who think the nation-state is not yet dead, the first formula cannot be entirely satisfactory. The second formula favouring national teams will be chosen, in the Japanese, French, or German ways.

Is the nation-state dead? Some states are more moribund than others, but for good or for ill, in spite of multinationals and the global economy, the institutional framework in which we live and work is still the nation-state with its laws and regulations, its taxes and benefits, its strengths and vicissitudes. We do not pay taxes to the United Nations, but to the federal, provincial and municipal governments. We are not paid in a world currency but in Canadian dollars. When we fall sick we use the Canadian Public Health System, not an international one. Quite apart from sentimental nationalism or its absence, all who receive paychecks in Canadian dollars have a vested interest in the health of the Canadian economy and the value of the Canadian dollar.

Studied indifference and pseudo-multinationalism is irrational. If Canadian firms fail, the repercussions will affect all of us through intricate macro-economic mechanisms. It would be foolish to take an aloof stance and pretend that as long as we can get foreign products cheaper we will be better off overall. Our ability to purchase these foreign products may become eroded if our economy ceases to be healthy.

To ignore the relevance of the nation-state, when we pay taxes to it and receive benefits from it, would be very unreasonable. Because of this continued relevance of the nation-state, it is foolhardy to ignore the differential effects of internal competition versus external competitiveness. Internal competition may yield short-term benefits for us as third-party consumers but external competitiveness will yield greater pay-offs in the long run. If that external competitiveness requires team play, because the rules of the international game have changed, we must not ignore that fact and live in a fool's paradise, repeating superficial clichés and quoting antiquated theories.

If the above analysis is correct, then a substantial rethinking of our competition and industrial policies is required. Competition policy in Canada, as in the United States, is to maximize competition for the benefit of consumers as third parties, to prevent monopolies and to keep firms small to medium-sized. Our fiscal incentives mechanisms favour smallness and punish bigness. We, therefore, tend to produce dynamic and enterprising economic dwarfs to do battle with equally dynamic and enterprising economic giants abroad; these giants, in addition, have their governments fully behind them.

The outcome can never be in doubt. The dwarfs score moral victories and the giants commercial ones. The pattern of Canadian innovation stops at good ideas. Lacking the wherewithal to make them happen, our good ideas tend to flow abroad and be re-imported as foreign products. The economic history of Canada is one long tale of missed opportunities, where lack of threshold effects has condemned new projects to still-birth. A consensus economy which would shift the locus and focus of competition from internal to external would probably lead to major positive results. It would unlock the handbrake which keeps the highly sophisticated and powerful Canadian engine from propelling us at more than middling velocities in world races.

Chapter 9

DOES CANADA HAVE
A MISSION STATEMENT ?

'Elan Vital' and Mission Statements.

Adversary systems tend to develop as an outgrowth of diverging interests. On the other hand, when there is a common purpose, or 'goal-congruence' as it is sometimes called in management circles, teamwork develops quite naturally. In Canada's case the relevant question is: how strong is the common purpose? What is its nature? Is it sufficiently-explicit to lead to consensus? This brings us to the other management notion of a 'mission statement' - the overall goal which gives a raison d'être to an organization. Without a mission statement, an organization, be it a firm, a government agency or an entire nation, cannot succeed. As the poet, Seneca, said, "There is no such thing as a favourable wind for he who knows not where he is going." Without a goal, a destination or a clear objective, the ship of state, in particular, will tend to drift in stormy seas, buffeted by turbulence and, ultimately, hitting the proverbial rocks.

Projet de société

The French have an even stronger expression of the 'mission statement' concept. It is called a *projet de société,* - literally a 'societal project', a vision of a desirable society towards which the nation should move. A *projet de société* is an articulate, explicit expression of where we want to be. The more explicit a *projet de société,* the more likely it is to be realized. In fact, its absence is often the cause of failure of social revolutions. The revolutionaries are quite clear about what they are *against ,* but often have no clue as to what they are *for* . After the revolution what? Unless that question can be meaningfully and precisely answered, the odds are that the revolution, whatever it is, will fail - or be replaced with a situation worse than the initial one which led to it.

Elan Vital

Another concept which goes hand-in-hand with mission statements and *projets de société* is *élan vital.* First developed by Henri Bergson in the late nineteenth century, the concept of élan vital is that of the life-force of a nation (or individual). It is the psychological energy that drives people and institutions. Its absence will doom even the best-designed organizations.

A version of élan vital was, in fact, developed by the late nineteenth century French strategic thinker, Arnaud du Picq. Applied to the military field, élan makes the basic difference between victory and defeat. Du Picq, a lecturer at the French war college, studied carefully the battles of the Ancient World. He tried to explain, for instance, why 300 Spartans could defeat 10,000 well-armed Persians at Thermopylae, or a handful of ships sink many times their opposing number at Salamis. Assuming the size differentials were historically confirmed and not the stuff of myths, something he verified to his satisfaction, du Picq arrived at his own version of élan, the "du Picq effect." Cavalry charging at each other to the sound of drums or bugles, claimed du Picq, was poetry not reality. In reality, in any frontal confrontation, one side attacks with élan and the other side is the passive victim of that élan. Battles are won and lost in the mind. The side with the psychological advantage, the greatest will to win, the strongest motivation, will triumph. When 300 can defeat 10,000 it is because the 10,000 are sitting around like passive sacrificial lambs. "It never troubles the wolf, how many the sheep are." The wolf has élan, the sheep enter quite quickly into the mind-set of victims.

Studies on victims and victimology have confirmed this idea of psychological pre-conditioning. A potential 'victim' exudes an air of vulnerability and helplessness. A non-victim communicates confidence and defiance. When the Americans were held hostage for many months in Teheran, in 1979-1980, a cartoon appeared in a North American newspaper showing a Russian leaning over the fence separating the American and Soviet embassies in Teheran. An American diplomat was asking him why it was that these things always seemed to happen to Americans and not to Russians. "Ah comrade," he said, "the answer is simple. We just don't allow that sort of thing!"

A related idea comes from the Japanese martial arts. Most of these martial arts, from Aikido to Judo and Karate are based on one fundamental premise: you do not defeat an adversary, *you create the conditions that will force him to defeat himself* . Judo and Aikido are constructed on the idea that an opponent's own élan, in this case, physical momentum, will be redirected against him. This allows a smaller to throw a much larger contestant, using the laws not only of physical but also of psychological leverage. In every judo throw, there is a preparatory 'tsukuri' phase and a final 'kake' phase. In the 'tsukuri' the designated victim will 'lose his balance' and makes himself vulnerable, by taking a step forward or backward or by shifting his weight from one foot to the other. With split-second timing, the martial arts expert exploits this minuscule imbalance and summons the laws of physics decisively to throw the opponent. This is the 'kake' or execution phase. However, without 'tsukuri' there can be no 'kake'. Without initial vulnerability there can be no defeat; conversely, without élan there can be no victory.

Another way to describe 'élan' is momentum. It is the acquired velocity that one has, for instance, in riding a sled down a steep hill or diving into a pool from a great height. The sense of speed is such that one feels it would take almost superhuman force to stop it.

Transposed to the psychology of individuals and nations, this dynamic momentum may spring from past successes and high achievement or from perceived major external threats. When the motivation levels are high enough, adrenalin pours into the individual's veins or those of the body-politic and performance reaches astonishing heights. Thus, at the individual level, Aikido masters have been known to dodge bullets and lift the backs of volkswagens to free a trapped child. With appropriate psychological motivation, non-swimmers have been known to jump in and save others on the point of drowning; patients with terminal illnesses have been known to rebound, order their immune systems into action and recover their health.

At the level of nations, small countries have been known to establish hegemony over much larger ones (Alexandrian Greece, Caesar's Rome and nineteenth-century Britain). Others have made their marks on world culture far exceeding their numbers (the Jewish people for instance). When élan vital is present, the Davids of this world can defeat all the Goliaths. Without élan, the superstars can succumb to third-rate opponents and defeat themselves into oblivion.

Does Canada have an élan vital? Does it have a clear *projet de société* ? Does it even have a discernible mission statement or raison d'être that would meet with the consensus of Canadians? *Canadians* have plenty of élan vital, but the country, as a whole, has much less. It seems to depend too much on the laws of inertia. It cannot be satisfactorily described to a curious foreigner who knows very little about the country. The attempted descriptions will tend to be purely factual, purely geographical, or anecdotal - the mission statement will not be readily forthcoming.

'Existential' Countries

Does a country really need a so-called 'mission statement' ? In Canada's case, the urgency comes from the challenge of continentalism, added to strong centrifugal forces. In fact, all viable countries have mission statements. Some are so obvious that it would be redundant to state them. A country with a long history and a strong national culture has the most unambiguous mission statement of all: *the preservation and enhancement of that culture.* When, however, the past is not a good guide to the future, because conditions have changed, a more explicit statement of purpose is needed. Otherwise, the country will fall into the category of what we can call 'existential nations'. Such a nation will continue to exist, due simply to inertia, until some major trauma challenges it. Then it will crumble and disintegrate.

An example of an 'existential country' was Austria-Hungary at the end of the nineteenth century. The ancient Habsburg Empire had evolved into a marriage of convenience, involving a multiracial, multicultural society. At the top of the multicultural 'totem pole' were the two charter cultures, German and Hungarian, sharing the condominium of power. Beneath that condominium simmered the national aspirations of no less than thirteen ethnic communities: Serbs, Croatians, Poles, Czechs, Slovaks, Bosnians, Herzegovinians and others.

As long as the weather map said 'sunny and warm', the Austro-Hungarian condominium muddled through. Vienna, its imperial capital, was the multicultural city par excellence - a gracious, highly civilized, highly cultured international city. However, the centrifugal forces of rival nationalist aspirations combined with the external trauma of the First World War sounded the death knell for Austria-Hungary.

The War itself was started when the Kronprinz Franz Ferdinand was assassinated by a nationalist Serb. This was the shot that plunged Europe into four years of murderous struggle, at the end of which, in the Versailles Treaty, the Austro-Hungarian Empire was dismembered. Its constituent nationalities each went their separate ways to become the mosaic of Eastern and Balkan Europe that we know today. The Empire revealed itself to have been existential. From about 1860 on, it survived on sheer inertia. Had there been no world war, it would have survived a few more years, perhaps a few decades. However, muddling through was not good enough for long-term existence. Without a clear mission, the country was bound to disintegrate - sooner or later.

An existential country may, then, be viewed as one which is likely to survive as long as there are no strong threats, internal or external, to jolt it; however, we would not bother inventing such a country if it did not already exist. As Montesquieu once wrote, "... Si le hasard d'une bataille, c'est à dire une cause particulière ruine un Etat, il y avait une cause générale qui faisait que cet Etat devait périr par une seule bataille." (*Grandeur et décadence des*

Romains, ch. XVIII) Or, "If the luck of one battle, that is, if a single cause brings about the ruin of a state, then there must have been a more general cause that dictated that the state must fall because of a single battle."

Canada's multi-ethnic similarities with Austria-Hungary are striking, including the condominium of two charter cultures. In addition, the 'existential' nature of Canada's confederation is becoming increasingly perplexing. The 'single battle' in Montesquieu's terminology, may turn out to be free trade and its sequels. Alternatively, it could be Quebec nationalism. But the possibility that either will lead to Canada's demise rests on the 'more general cause' of centrifugal forces and lack of common purpose.

Canada's Need for a Mission Statement

As a rule, the need for a mission statement is directly proportional to the existence of competing alternatives to a present structure. Robinson Crusoe did not bother to define himself on his desert island because he had no one else to relate to. The European Community has to define itself if it is ever going to transcend the chauvinism of its member states. Similarly, Canada must define itself, precisely because the external challenge of continentalism is now about to reach its strongest point. The onus of proof is on Canadians to show that they are not merely Ontarians, Quebecers, Newfoundlanders, Albertans - or Algomans. There must be something that unites all in a minimum common purpose, which is different from that of our southern neighbour. If it is not different, then there is no reason in the world to remain separate, when all forces beckon us to merge.

Many countries find their mission statements in the preservation of a deep national culture. The condition for that kind of a mission statement is a strong history, full of events which may be remembered and cherished and a number of traditions, ways of life, cultural folkways and mores, that we can associate with that country.

There must even be a few stereotypes to reinforce the common purpose. For instance, there are a number of attributes which we can readily associate with the adjectives 'British', 'French', 'German' or 'Italian'. To say that such a behaviour is 'typically French' or 'typically German' or 'typically Italian' is to be quite understandable. The stereotypes are obviously exaggerations but, like a good caricature, they stress a feature which we identify with the object of the caricature. They enlarge upon connotations not just denotations. These cultures have what would be called in the language of the theatre 'stage-presence'. You can feel them. You can see them. You can cut them with a knife, they are so real.

One of the major characteristics of contemporary Canada - that is both an asset and a source of weakness - *is the absence of an exciting history.* By comparative world standards, we have not had a very eventful past. Fortunately, on the human side, we have few battles to remember, few martyrs to lament. However, this also means that we have few revolutions to celebrate and few monuments to rally around. Most of the battles that were fought and are celebrated in Canadian history were connected with the Franco-British struggle for dominance (The Plains of Abraham); or with some incidents in the War of 1812 with the United States, that we prefer to forget in order to show our friendship with our southern neighbour; or a few twentieth century engagements fought under the British Flag to protect Europe (Dieppe, Vimy Ridge). Once these are dealt with, Canadian history is not particularly exciting, either to study or to teach. One rapidly gets tired of the cod, the fur trade and the settlement of the land by *coureurs de bois*. There are no industrial revolutions to analyse, Napoleonic Wars to assess, a Bismarck to study or a Garibaldi to admire. Consequently, when we strive to reflect Canada's heritage, there is an obvious temptation to stress the natural world and to give precedence to geography. One is reminded, once again, of John A. Macdonald's statement that Canada has too much geography and not enough history!

The Ottawa Hull Region is, in some senses, too successful in its task of reflecting Canada. The Gamma Institute conducted a two-year study for the National Capital Commission to explore how best to make Ottawa-Hull a true national capital. Certain important conclusions emerged. The first was that when people were asked how they felt about their national capital their answer was not at all what one would normally expect. If Italians are asked how they feel about Rome, they will answer that they either hate it or love it. The same is true of the Frenchman about Paris or the Englishman about London. What was striking about the Canadian responses was that the majority answered that they were totally indifferent to Ottawa and really could not care less! Neither strong feelings of opposition nor strong admiration were voiced. No élan was shown, one way or the other. The second significant perception of the Ottawa-Hull Region was that it is, by almost unanimous vote, a very pleasant place in which to live. It is "nice and quiet", "clean and green" and in so being may, inadvertently, reflect one image of Canada, that of a rather dull but pleasant expanse of land. That Ottawa is considered a nice place to live in but not such a 'hot' place to visit, runs counter to the traditional perception of most national capitals, where the opposite is said. "They are fascinating places to visit, but who would want to live there?" When National Capital Commission officials privately confided to me, a few years ago, that they did not know what to do with visitors staying more than two days in the National Capital Region, that was a telling statement of the weakness of Canada's current *projet de société* .

We need a mission statement, then, and an eloquent one at that. We need it because, first, there is an alternative to Canada - the United States. This is an alternative that some will find more and more attractive as the continental economy completes its integration process. Again, it should be repeated that Canada's sole original mission statement was the 'not-America' theme, bolstered by the European link.

The second reason why we need a mission statement is the continuing possibility of Quebec separation. Quebec nationalism alternates, as we have argued in a previous chapter, between a latent state and a radical state. In a radical state, the objective is an expansion of Quebec's autonomy, expressed in slogans such as "maîtres chez nous", the motto of the Quiet Revolution or "souveraineté-association". The latent state is defensive in nature and has, as its principal objective, the preservation of 'acquired rights' and a vigilance to ensure that what Ottawa has given with one hand, it will not take away with the other. The predominance of the French language in Quebec and its near-equal status on the federal scene are among these 'acquired rights'.

We should open a parenthesis here on the question of the possible effects of free trade on Quebec nationalism. One view holds that the very notion of free trade is antithetical to that of nationalism and that Quebec's support for free trade, in 1988, was evidence of the end of separatism. This view is actually quite superficial. The opposite view, that free trade may well reinforce Quebec nationalism - or at least weaken Quebec's stake in Canada - has greater credibility. A number of Quebec intellectuals are either already asking, or will ask in the near future, the following question, "*Now that we have free trade with the United States, why does Quebec still need Canada?* "

If Canada had a strong mission statement, the answer would be obvious. But, in the absence of such a *projet de société,* the question is thorny, especially if one factors in Meech Lake. As we have seen, Meech Lake will have, as one of its overall effects, the transfer of power from the federal government to the provinces. This will give added weight to the question, "*What can Ottawa do for Quebec that Quebec cannot do for itself?* " In addition, one must note the continuing resentment of some radical Quebec nationalists, whose emotional attachment to Canada is nil. As some Québecois have expressed it: "Now that we cannot be sovereign Québecois, frankly we would rather be American, (or even Mexican) than Canadian." Quebec nationalism, strong, vibrant and possessing its own *projet de société* - the preservation of Quebec's French character, culture and traditions faces a much weaker and more difficult-to-define pan-Canadian nationalism.

New Canadians

The third, and perhaps most important, reason for a strong mission statement for Canada is the demographic shift away from the charter cultures to "New Canadians" from countries other than Britain and France. While immigration was primarily confined to nationals of the two mother countries of Britain and France, the situation was

different. Some claim that one of the strengths of Canada
is precisely the absence of a mission statement, its 'mosaic'
rather than its 'melting pot', its lack of homogeneity and its
great tolerance for diversity. This is, to some extent, true
and such virtues are, indeed, desirable.

But, when all is said and done, 'diversity' may not
be enough to hold the country together. By the year 2,000,
a combination of low birthrates and high immigration from
Latin America, Asia and Africa will change the ethnic
composition of Canada. In 1988, between a quarter and a
third of all Canadians claimed ancestry from other than
charter cultures. By the year 2,000, this proportion will
exceed 50 percent. The 'typical' Canadian, in the year
2,000, will have a lineage traceable neither to Montcalm
nor to Wolfe. This typical Canadian will have immigrated
from remote places around the globe and will have little
empathy with the kings of England and France and what
they did, or did not do, to Canada.

The immigrant wishes to integrate. But what does
integration mean in the absence of a common purpose? In
Quebec, integration means speaking French and an
adherence to what is emerging as a 'Quebec way of life'.
Does that mean the same thing as 'integration' in Alberta,
British Columbia or the Maritimes? Ontario, probably the
most multicultural province of Canada, is a window on the
future. As long as the Ontario economy is healthy, all its
various cultures will work, in English primarily, to
maintain and expand it. However, if there are signs of
trouble, the unintegrated cultural groupings will fall back
upon themselves and eye one another with suspicion. In
the absence of the nation-wide *projet de société* , our new
immigrants will simply not integrate. While their cousins
in the United States will become full-fledged Americans,

they will retain their original identities, with a vengeance, by attempting to create replicas of the old country: Little Italy, Little Portugal, Little Greece, and so on. Ultimately, as the common purpose of 'Canada' becomes more and more nebulous, the new Canadians will look with increasing favour to continental political union, which will reunite them with their cousins from the old country, probably currently living in California or Chicago.

Immigrants tend to fall into two categories. The first perceives Canada as a stepping stone to somewhere else. This 'somewhere else' may either be the United States or a return to the old country, having made one's fortune. This group will tend to be only minimally involved in Canadian issues and will stay clear of Canadian politics. Its members are really 'émigrés' rather than immigrants. For this first group, a North American Economic Union is an excellent opportunity and a Canada/United States merger quite desirable.

The second category includes those immigrants who are more bullish about Canada than the 'old' Canadians who have been here for many generations. This second group has high expectations of this country. Its demands are high and it is willing to offer a great deal in return. It is the group most likely to be frustrated by the 'shilly-shallying' and lack of purpose that it perceives in Canada. Once that group becomes disaffected, it will join the first and lose any emotional attachment to the country, choosing instead pragmatic opportunism. In addition, disaffected immigrants will seek to return to their roots. Hence, they will explore cultural ancestry and remain more attached to their original motherlands than to the new one. Alternatively, in generation number two, they will allow themselves to be captured by the myths and fantasies associated with the 'American way of life' and become more American than Canadian.

The arrival of new waves of immigration in the nineties, combined with a probable renaissance of active Quebec nationalism, both stemming from the current feebleness of Canada's purpose, will obviously increase the strength of the centrifugal forces in the country. At the limit, what may result is a progressive 'balkanization' of the land, with the fragmentation of the nation into multiple distinct societies. From that, a *Ghetto Canada* may emerge. The implications of this are immense, and we will examine them in the concluding chapter.

For all theses reasons then, we strongly believe that Canada's mission statement, raison d'être, *projet de société* or what have you, should be clarified and made explicit, if the country is, in the long run, to stay together.

On what should a Canadian
PROJET DE SOCIÉTÉ be based?

With no strong myths to bind it together, Canada has experienced, and will experience, difficulties in defining itself. However, the opportunity is there and the country has sufficient positive potential for greatness to allow it to move towards a clear destination. Here again, as Richard Gwyn points out, the presence of a competing American culture is a strong challenge. The cultural influence of the United States is almost as strong as its economic influence. In 1985, 75 percent of the viewing-time of English Canadians was occupied with U.S. programmes. Ninety-seven percent of movies watched originated in the United States. (*The 49th Paradox*, p. 141) In contrast, the demand for Canadiana, in all its forms, is weak. There is a minority audience interested in Canada;

books dealing with this country have a much smaller chance of becoming best-sellers than cook-books, human interest stories or biographies of American politicians.

On the other hand, Canadian activities in the cultural field are very strong. Toronto, for instance, supports forty-two theatre groups, third in the English-speaking world after London and New York. Montréal is a capital of arts, leisure and entertainment and summer in this city is one long succession of world-class international festivals. It is not for want of culture that Canada has a weak mission statement, but more for want of a unified culture or network of cultures.

In order to construct and reinforce the raison d'être of Canada a number of building blocks must be considered. A short list includes the following four: The 'other-than-America' theme, 'transculturalism', the pursuit of national excellence and social and environmental innovation. Let us examine the potential of each in turn.

1. The 'Not-America' Theme

The 'not-America' theme is likely to remain central to the Canadian identity unless the country enters into a political federation with the United States. Indeed, without some kind of 'other-than-America' theme, there is little reason to justify a border at the 49th parallel. As we have seen, the historical 'not-America' theme was strongly linked to a European connection, which gave body and credibility to that difference. In the same way that Quebec wishes to be a 'distinct' society within Canada, Canada must maintain a 'distinctiveness' with respect to the United States. Without a clear-cut distinctiveness, Canada is likely to become nothing more than a hinterland for the United States heartland. In a North America where everything is the same, the comparative advantages of the region called 'Canada' will not be easy to identify and to sell. Too many factors favour the concentration of activity in the centre and south of the continent. The 'not-America' theme must remain a rallying point for the country, but must be given new forms. If it is negative and defensive, it will fail. If it is positive and celebratory, it will succeed. It must be a kind of distinctiveness that Americans would applaud as much as Canadians do, prompting them to say, "*vive la différence!* " This 'différence' could be based on a combination of the following three building blocks.

2. Transculturalism

Multiculturalism, in the Canadian context, is the preservation and enhancement of differences between the various cultures that make up modern Canada. Multiculturalism is very worthwhile, but in its simple form it is a double-edged sword, since it can increase centrifugal forces and make the Ghetto Canada scenario real. If strong walls are built to protect every ethnic community in Canada, it will not be surprising if we arrive at a mosaic, not of cultures, but of rival fiefdoms, characterized by spheres of interest, block-voting and ultimately perhaps, ethnic strife - not just between French and English but among all groups. The two solitudes will become three, six or even sixteen.

The flip-side of multiculturalism is what we have called, at the Gamma Institute, 'transculturalism'. In multiculturalism, cultures are superimposed upon each other, but remain quite separate. *There are no bridges between them* . At one extreme, there is the straight melting pot. In that scenario, all immigrant cultures are put in the blender and coloured by the dominant culture of the host country; what comes out is a regimented replication of similar individuals, all adhering to the same set of values.

At the other extreme is indiscriminate multiculturalism, where the only commonality is distinctiveness and separation. If Canada wants to recreate the United Nations within its territory, it will likely succeed as well as the United Nations - unfortunately a forum more of discord than of consensus.

Enter 'transculturalism'. Transculturalism, like multiculturalism, preserves identities and roots but adds *communication between the cultures to create new valuable syntheses.* A transcultural nation will, as the name implies, *transcend* its component cultures and reach new heights of achievement. Above all, such a nation would possess a majority of transcultural individuals who are equally at ease in many cultures. This is a tremendous opportunity for Canada, perhaps its best.

Canadian Prime Ministers, such as Pierre Elliot Trudeau and Brian Mulroney, are examples of transcultural individuals. Speaking accentless French and English, they are not only equally at ease in both languages but, more importantly, probably think in both.

Language is the prime vehicle of thought. To speak French is not just to be able to know that 'jaune' means 'yellow', but to be conversant with the French intellectual style and imbued with the logico-deductive Cartesian approach.

Similarly, to speak English is not just to be able to say 'hello' instead of 'bonjour', but to understand and internalize the Anglo-American intellectual style - in turn imbued with empiricism, pragmatism and directness. The combination of the two styles - not just languages - gives a considerable competitive advantage to such individuals. In a country of monocultural individuals, the bi-cultural individual will most likely form the élite.

If biculturalism confers an advantage, transculturalism, which may involve more than two cultures, confers an even greater one. Transcultural immigrants to Canada will be able to speak not only English and French perfectly, but their native tongues too. They will, therefore, be the heirs to at least three intellectual styles, not two, and will be enriched by as many different cultures. Extend the process further and introduce transculturalism as a national policy. Then you breed creative excellence in individuals who become the locus of integration of three, four, five cultures - the theoretical limit, linguists tell us, being much higher than what we commonly believe.

Transcultural individuals tend not only to be culturally versatile but also very creative. *Transculturalism breeds entrepreneurship, a commodity which Canada presently squanders.* Canadian entrepreneurs, discouraged by the brakes created by multiple adversary systems, are tempted to emigrate to the United States or Europe. But the potentially transcultural character of the country certainly does breed them.

Here an important allied fact must be taken into consideration. Studies have shown that, in most countries, immigrants are more motivated to become entrepreneurs than native-born citizens. There are at least two reasons for this. First, the immigrant is the 'new kid on the block' and must try harder to survive, while the native-born citizen enjoys the complacency of a comfortable, structured existence. But secondly, immigrants bring with them cultural bags of tricks which they can make good use of in the host country, especially if they combine them with local cultural themes. Thus Italian-American pizza was born of a marriage between the coarser Neapolitan pizza of

Italy and the need to adapt it to American palates. This American pizza ended-up being re-exported to Europe and Italy as a new hybrid product. The same is true for other food products, such as chop suey (which did not exist in China), the Greco-American 'souvlak' sandwich, Lebanese-American specialities, and 'le T-Bone avec sauce bearnaise'.

Above and beyond individual new products born of transculturalism, we have major entrepreneurial successes. Indians and Pakistanis have been more successful entrepreneurs in Anglophone Africa, Britain and Canada than in their native countries. French-speaking Vietnamese immigrants have come into their own in France, Quebec and Francophone Africa; they seem to have achieved less in their own country, where the Chinese have traditionally been strong. The Lebanese and Armenians have a long history of success in their respective diasporas. The Italian entrepreneurs, dormant in Italy in the first half of this century, have exploded with vitality in North America. The Chinese, themselves, meeting limited success as entrepreneurs in mainland China have, abroad, dominated the economies they have penetrated. In three out of the four 'Mini-Dragons' of Southeast Asia` - Taiwan, Hong Kong and Singapore - the Chinese are the major entrepreneurs. In less recent history, the migration of Greeks and Jews from Constantinople, after its fall in 1453, is believed by some historians to have triggered the Italian Renaissance. In turn, the Italian Renaissance was exported to the rest of Europe by Italian entrepreneurs, bringing economic development to Spain and Flanders and making these areas financial and banking centres.

The dialectic clash of cultures has, historically, produced hybrid forms which are richer than the initial component parts. Therefore, transculturalism is a major 'ace-in-the-hole' for Canada. How can Canada best make use of it?   The essence of transculturalism is communication between cultures - the bridge effect. In policy terms, the enabling principle would, therefore, be quite simple. *All multicultural programmes should have a transcultural component - that is, every programme that reinforces an ethnic identity should be complemented by a second programme which facilitates bridging, communication and synthesis with other ethnic groups .*

3. <u>The Pursuit of National Excellence</u>

The third possible building block in Canada's *projet de société* is the pursuit of excellence on the global scene - going for the gold, not just the bronze.   Why should that pursuit keep the country together? For the simple reason that nothing succeeds like success and nothing fails like failure. If a country is a going concern, no one will think of tearing it up.

The Swiss have taught us this valuable lesson. Switzerland is multi-ethnic, with Swiss-Germans, Swiss-Italians and Swiss-Frenchmen occupying different parts of the country. There is no particular great love or undying affection between each of these sub-groups, who will regularly joke about each other and remain socially separate.   However, because Switzerland is very successful, there are no separatist movements to speak of. The Swiss work together to achieve a common purpose: the preservation of the Swiss institutions that have brought wealth and success to the country. The sub-groups need not be madly in love with each other to keep the country going and achieve qualitative excellence in many fields.

The same principle could apply to Canada. A *successful* Canada would be claimed by all Canadians.

The majority would reject a mediocre Canada, and blame the mediocrity on others. A striking example of this phenomenon is in the area where Canada has claimed and achieved world-class excellence - ice hockey. When Team Canada beat the Soviet Union, on that memorable day, in September 1972, at the end of the first Canada-Russia Hockey Series, the crowds of revellers on Ste. Catherine Street in Montreal forgot who was French and who was English. Everyone was Canadian. The nationalism was celebratory and joyful. When Canada loses, on the other hand, everyone seeks to blame the other. There is a tendency to dissociate oneself from losers, to assign blame, to disparage, to accuse.

If Canada had ten things like hockey - genuine Canadian inventions where Canada maintains world-class excellence - there would be no need for explicit mission statements or societal projects. Everything would be clear. A corporate culture of success is a tremendous motivator for the private sector. Similarly a national culture of success could be a tremendous tonic for Canada. Unfortunately, we have not worked hard enough to create these ten 'hockey clones'. In some cases, we have had genuine Canadian inventions, which were world class but which we hastened to export, only to see them exploited by others.

The word processor, for instance, was, for all practical purposes, invented in Canada. However, Canada quickly lost its advantage and allowed the invention to be brought to fruition elsewhere. Canada's interactive videotext, the Telidon, was a state-of-the-art machine in 1980-81. Once again, the advantage was frittered away. So was the STOL aircraft and countless other products of Canadian creativity. What is also distressing is that our best minds often choose to go elsewhere. Among the best known world-class Canadians were Marshall McLuhan, John Kenneth Galbraith and, in 1989, the "Great One", Wayne Gretzky, all expatriates to the United States. Before the Quiet Revolution, there was even a saying in Quebec that, "the money goes to the United States, the brains go to France and the Vatican takes the rest".

A concerted Canadian policy to encourage excellence could be a powerful antidote to centrifugal forces. It could keep the country together in a much more significant fashion than dozens of legally-complicated constitutions.

4. Social and Environmental Innovation

Among the major candidates for 'made-in-Canada' excellence are a number of areas of social and environmental innovation: eco-development, health and welfare systems, high technology with a human face, educational psychology and a general forward-looking stance.

Social innovation is the implementation of new ways of doing things, new policies, new management structures at the level of the nation. Canada can achieve its distinctiveness through the development of this theme. If the past is not vivid enough to get the adrenalin flowing, perhaps anticipating and shaping the future is.

The first candidate area of social innovation is eco-development. This concept describes an economic and social development in harmony with the physical environment. The destruction of our ecosystem is a major planetary concern. Whether we are talking about acid rain, the greenhouse effect and climate change or toxic wastes causing disease, the physical environment is part of our lives. To ignore it is to court ruin. Political awareness of our ecosystem is now steadily increasing and it is quite possible that, in the future, elections will be won or lost on this issue. Canada has been ,traditionally, strong in this area. One thinks here of the important work of Maurice Strong, and of Christian de Laet in the conceptualization of the questions involved. In addition, in the early seventies, Canada developed the concept of *the Conserver Society* (at the Science Council and the Gamma Institute) and was a regular contributor to the international debate on the limits to growth. Managing our ecosystem and creating appropriate structures to live in harmony with nature would be an excellent way of making a virtue out of necessity - since we have too much geography and too little history, let us be pioneers in managing that geography in an optimal fashion.

Another area of possible social innovation is health and welfare. We claim that, as a nation, 'we care'. What that means is that we have established safety nets for the preservation of the health of our citizens and the enhancement of their welfare that are international showcases. We can build more systematically on these themes and innovate further. This might also include a major effort in humanizing technology, giving our high-tech society a human face, once again as a showcase to the world. The short list of possible building blocks for Canadian *projets de société* could become as long as we want. The themes could be multiplied indefinitely. The challenge is to find areas of endeavour which can mobilize the national will, be credible, 'made-in-Canada' social innovations and have a good chance of achieving world-class excellence. Once we have enough of these building blocks, national self-doubt and identity crises will be nothing more than amusing historical souvenirs

Chapter 10

CONCLUSION:
SCENARIOS AND STRATEGIES

A Summary of the Analysis

Canada is a country superbly endowed with human and natural resources, yet somehow unable to 'put it all together'. Because of its inability to meet its two major challenges, the external and the internal, the country is condemning itself to mediocrity, to middling performance, to 'bronze medals'.

The external challenge is, in one sentence, coping with the United States. The 'Hesitation Waltz' of the past century-and-a-half has bred approach/avoidance, love/hate, admiration and fear. Geographical, economic and technological forces point to closer union with the United States. Yet, there is still a strong desire to maintain the country - separate and independent. Making the two goals compatible is at the heart of the external challenge.

The internal challenge, in one sentence, is the difficulty of keeping this country together, given the centrifugal forces that pull it apart. Our mode of governance and our economic game-plan are based on the virtues of individual competition, in a world that has become group-competitive, without informing us of this fact through official channels. In this group-competitive world, where teams blow individuals right out of the water, we continue to go our merry way: the 'feds' against the provincials, business against the civil servants, workers against managers and lilliputian firms struggling for microscopic advantage in the 'little league', while the big boys abroad make it to the 'playoff finals'. The multiple adversarial systems, which we have created, act as a locked handbrake negating the abundant horsepower of the national engine. And beneath it all is a singular lack of common purpose, the absence of a mission statement - or better still, of a 'vision' statement - to bind the country together.

Yet, there is no denying that 'gold' is available. Which other country enjoys such resource abundance relative to its population, such a diversified human and cultural base, stands at the confluence of the American, Atlantic and Pacific worlds and enjoys such a positive external image?

The report card on Canada's past performance is therefore mixed: fair to good in absolute terms; among the better performances in the family of nations, yet but a fraction of the potential. Where, then, does the future lead us?

The political situation at the dawn of the nineties can be visualized in terms of an unequal struggle between two sets of forces, as reflected in Figure 4. In this configuration, six powerful 'meltdown' forces oppose three much weaker 'forces of national unity'. The diagram depicts the 'assault' of blocks 'B' (increasing divergences between Quebec and English Canada), 'C' (adversary systems), 'D' (weakening of the central government) against the three defensive forces, 'F' (inertia and historical tradition), 'G', (remaining socio-cultural differences between the United States and Canada and 'H' (whatever remains of the political will to defend the country).

However, the order of battle shows the defensive forces about to be outflanked by two irresistible bulldozers: Block 'E' (accelerating North American integration) and Block 'A' (the erosion of Canada's raison d'être). If the outflanking were to succeed, the defensive forces would have been defeated and Canada would become ungovernable.

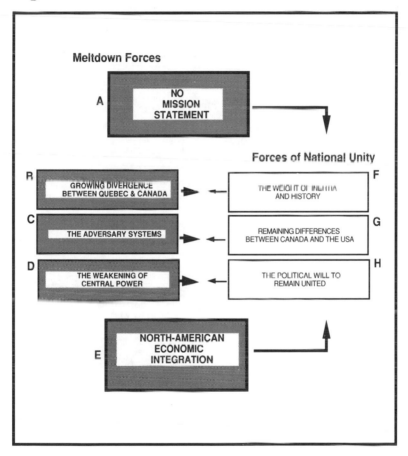

Figure 4
Canada, circa 1990
The Order of Battle

The interplay between these six forces may eventually lead to the following four scenarios as depicted in Figure 5 and described in detail below.

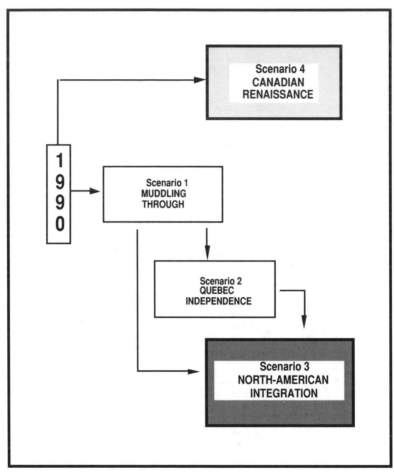

Figure 5
Four Plausible Scenarios

Scenario 1 : Muddling Through

The 'Muddling Through' scenario is an extension of the status quo. It is not a disaster scenario since, for all intents and purposes, Canada has survived and to a certain extent thrived with this mode of governance. Doomsayers and disaster-mongers should, therefore, be kept in check.

The end of the world is not upon us, even with 'muddling through'. But 'muddling through' is distinctly sub-optimal, and probably not viable in the longer run, because of changed economic and geopolitical conditions.

The basic characteristic of this scenario is that public policy remains reactive rather than proactive and somehow 'lets the river flow', hoping that things will sort themselves out. It is reminiscent of what has been known as 'Mustapha's Law', in some management circles: *if you do nothing about a problem long enough it will go away.*

'Muddling Through' is leaving as many things as possible implicit, rather than explicit, to avoid offending any one group, and improvising compromises here and there to meet with crises as they come along. Born negotiators thrive on 'muddling through', because they are experts in the art of the compromise. But born negotiators do not necessarily make good statesmen. In fact, there is evidence that they make bad statesmen, because of their propensity to say *après moi le déluge.* "Let us negotiate a deal now and the h *** with the consequences. In the long run, we will all be dead anyway!" The doctrine of 'management by exception' leads the ship of state.

In the 'Muddling Through' scenario, relations with the United States follow the historical patterns of the 'Hesitation Waltz'. There is no clear will to move into a common market and/or economic union with our southern neighbour, nor to be a different society. As a result, half-measures abound. The conventional clichés return and the pendulum swings back and forth between approach and avoidance.

On the internal front, the centrifugal forces gain the upper hand. The provincial level of government becomes increasingly dominant. At the federal level, monetary

policy is still a potent instrument, but the Canadian dollar
is now so closely tied to the U.S. that it is, for all intents
and purposes, the same currency with different coloring on
the paper. On the fiscal side, tax reform and transfers of
spending power to the provinces leave the federal
government as one player among many in the Canadian
public sector, with a spending clout that can go down to
only about 20 percent of all public sector spending, the rest
belonging to the other levels of government. Inter-
provincial rivalry is maximized, with each province
competing alone against all the others, trying to obtain a
larger share of the' pie'.

The new Canada of highly diversified ethnic
composition with non-British, non-French, new Canadians
now the majority, develops into cultural enclaves or
cantons. There is 'balkanization' and a 'Ghetto Canada'
emerges. Every community jealously guards its autonomy
in the fashion of medieval lords controlling the manor.
Central authority is symbolic. There is no attempt to target
or select national goals and the recognition of diversity
becomes the *modus operandi* . Beyond well-worn clichés,
there is no mission statement around which to rally or to
get excited.

The 'Muddling Through' scenario raises three
questions. First, has Canada always been muddling
through or is it a recent phenomenon? Second, if the latter,
when did we fall into this mode? Third, whether desirable
or not, how viable, in the long run, is 'muddling through'?

To the first question we answer that, in some
senses, Canada has been muddling through from its very
inception. We must, however, qualify that by saying that
there are degrees of depth and density of the muddle. In
the period from the end of the French Régime, in 1763, to

Confederation, Canada's membership in the most powerful empire on earth was a sufficiently-clear purpose to make 'muddling through' work. After the repeal of the British Corn Laws in 1846, the signing of the Reciprocity Treaty with the United States and the formation of British North America in 1867, the density of the muddle increased somewhat, but remained still manageable. Until about 1956, which marks the irreversible decline of the British Empire, the European counterweight and a generally-favourable international economy allowed 'muddling through' to remain eminently feasible and a plausible strategy for a country like Canada.

In the sixties, things began to change. The Quiet Revolution in Quebec led to radical Quebec nationalism, while increased integration with the United States and the globalization of the international economy began to upset the delicate equilibrium. The seventies were spent fighting Quebec separatism and attempting to resurrect the European connection, with the aborted 'special relationship' that Canada sought to implement with the EEC. The decade was also spent reacting to world-wide stagflation.

At the beginning of the eighties, the severe recession, of 1981-1982, hurt Canada badly but the patriation of the Constitution and the temporary defeat of Quebec separatism created a new situation. Much of the eighties were spent enjoying the Wall Street Bull Market and riding on the coat-tails of the U.S. recovery, itself fuelled by foreign loans and enormous fiscal deficits. An early version of the Meech Lake Accord was signed in October 1987, and the Free Trade Agreement came into force in January 1989. These and other events, such as the Crash of October 1987, the resurrection of Quebec nationalism and the international rethinking of the role of the state have deepened the 'muddle' considerably. In December 1988, new language tensions arose in Quebec and ethnic polarization began to increase over this sensitive issue.

In our view, although 'muddling through' has worked, in the past, to maintain Canada in some form of equilibrium, *it is not viable in the long run. Its life expectancy is not likely to extend past the nineties.*

At about the end of the nineties, the combined forces of centrifugality within Canada and continentalism will make alternative choices much more attractive. The vagueness of the national mission statement, allied to the coming of many new immigrants and the drawing apart of existing communities within Canada, will force a choice. We will either have to accept and work towards a deeper continentalism and envision what is presently unthinkable - political union with the United States - or try to build the nation to a level of self-confidence and excellence that will keep it viable, indefinitely.

Scenario 2 : Quebec Separation.

Quebec separation from Canada was a strong possibility in the seventies. The movement fell out of fashion in the eighties but, in our view, is scheduled to be a strong force in the nineties. To gain a perspective on the issue, it should be pointed out that, had the 1980 Quebec Referendum been handled like the 'Free Trade Election' of 1988, *Quebec would already have been entitled to declare its independence!* What saved the "No" forces, in 1980, was that they were united under one banner - by law. This turned out to be a strategic mistake for the Parti Québécois. Had it scheduled a 'referendum-election', citing British parliamentary tradition, it would have won.

(British parliamentary tradition does not favour referenda on specific issues, but rather elections even when one issue is dominant.) Had the "No" vote been divided, as it was on the free trade issue, in 1988, between the Liberals and the New Democrats, the "Yes" vote, in 1980, would have won the day. Conversely, had there been a national referendum on free trade in 1988, the "No" side would have won.

The independence movement in Quebec is gaining strength from at least four quarters. First, there is the question of Meech Lake - at the time of writing still unsigned. If Meech Lake becomes the law of the land, then the decentralizing forces will gain the upper hand and provincial power will become much stronger than federal power. This will make the federal government less relevant to Quebec and enhance the independence position. If, on the other hand, Meech Lake is not signed, or is significantly modified, or is repealed later, then the bitterness in Quebec may be very high and many disgruntled Quebecers will seek solace in the Parti Québécois or other independence parties.

Second, there is the question of language. This issue has now become a 'red hat' question in Quebec, to use the expression of Edward de Bono in *Six Thinking Hats* (London: Penguin, 1985). A 'red' thinking hat means that the discussion on an issue has become totally emotional and rational discourse very difficult to achieve (a white hat being neutrality, a green hat the search for alternatives and a black hat systematic negativism). The 'red hat' aspect of language in Quebec splits the debaters down the middle, according to ethnicity and not political ideology. Francophones, whether Conservative, Liberal or NDP, overwhelmingly believe that strong and coercive language legislation is the only way to protect French, threatened with extinction, and that Quebec Anglophones already enjoy a privileged status - as minorities go. For the Anglophones, the question is not one of language, but rather of human rights and democratic principles. The tension that results from this dispute fans the flames of separatism. (By the way, such disputes are not an exclusively Canadian problem, since language tensions are even stronger in Belgium, Switzerland and the Catalan region in Spain.) We are now seeing a Quebec that is increasingly unilingual French and a rest-of-Canada that is increasingly unilingual English. If this present direction continues, the lines of separation will become even clearer.

Third, there is the question of international representation. Quebec has, over the years, slowly raised its international profile and has acquired some attributes of international recognition as a sovereign state. Since Lesage, Quebec sometimes refers to itself as a 'state' and even more often, as a 'nation'. The Quebec legislature is known as the 'National Assembly' and when one casually refers to the 'national government', odds are that people think of the one in Québec City, not in Ottawa. Quebec Houses abroad (les "Maisons du Québec") are mini-embassies and in some countries compete in size with Canadian embassies. Quebec's relationship with other governments in Canada has been handled by a series of departments whose names, on the symbolic level, are telling: "intergovernmental affairs", "international affairs", Generally speaking, the federal government is sometimes referred to as the "Canadian" government, in the same way that one can talk about the "Italian" or the "Mexican" government.

Fourth, there is the question of free trade and its impact on Quebec nationalism. As was pointed out elsewhere, free trade is, paradoxically, an enhancer of nationalism - at least in the short run. The basic argument is simple. Quebec may belong to either or both of two 'clubs', the Canadian and/or the American. With Meech Lake and centrifugal forces, the Canadian club will have less and less to offer, while the U.S. club, at least at the economic level, can offer considerably more. Therefore, the question arises: why does Quebec still need Canada now that free trade is a fact?

Finally, the lack of a coherent, meaningful and adrenalin-inducing Canadian *projet de société*, amplifies the first four arguments for independence and will lead new generations of Quebecers seriously to ask themselves the "Why Canada?" question. From "what does Quebec want?" the perennial question of the seventies, will come the question of the nineties: "What can Canada give us that we do not have already?"

Scenario 3 : Continental Destiny.

The Continental Destiny scenario involves ultimate political union with the United States. The scenario assumes the economic success of free trade, and its spillover into a North American customs union and common market, with free movements of factors of production, including population, in both directions. The slow, creeping continentalism of the past, somewhat compatible with the 'muddling-through' option, is about to be replaced by galloping continentalism. This will entail the full acceleration of economic, technological and demographic integrating trends, as was seen in earlier chapters. By the turn of the new century, the economic union could also become a political union. Canadian provinces would then become U.S. states, with possible rearrangements and consolidations in Canada, prior to that merger. A special deal may be negotiated to ease the transition and Canada could be recognized as a 'distinct society' following the signature and approval of a continental version of the Meech Lake Accord - but probably negotiated this time in Camp David, Maryland.

The Continental Destiny scenario raises a number of questions. The first is, why would the United States accept to integrate Canada into its political system? An invitation was indeed handed out, in 1775, and it has been backed by military action twice since! But the United States of the 1990s is unlikely to covet territorial expansionism in North America, because there is little to gain. For all intents and purposes, it has already obtained whatever it needs from Canada.

From the point of view of the United States, *a docile, friendly and quiet Canada* is the best possible scenario, not a Canada that is part of the United States, unless certain conditions make political absorption desirable. What could these conditions be? *A turbulent, restless and hostile Canada* would be dangerous for the United States, and if the conditions for ending this restlessness were full absorption then so be it. The United States would be reluctant, but would ultimately accept.

A Canada-United States merger would also provide a land-bridge linking Alaska to the other states in the union - certainly a desirable objective from the U.S. point of view. In addition, a new United States of America, of truly continental proportions and endowed with many of the riches of the earth, would be a formidable economic adversary for any other bloc, European or Asian. It would be a geopolitician's dream and could conceivably reverse the process of the decline of the United States.

From Canada's point of view, political union with the United States would, of course, mean undoing the raison d'être of Canada. It would not be a 'fate worse than death' as some people claim, but it would mean a definite change in the lives of all Canadians.

What would probably happen is that the United States would recognize most, but not all, Canadian provinces as U.S. states and perhaps allow them slightly more autonomy than their U.S. counterparts, for a transitionary period. In addition, a population exchange would be very likely. A number of Canadians would cross the 49th parallel and fulfil childhood dreams of moving to California, Florida or Texas, lured by higher salaries, lower taxes, green fields, beaches and sun.

At the same time, a number of Americans would probably move north of the border in search of the 'new frontier' that Canada would represent. The western frontier was a determining feature of the culture of nineteenth century America. It channelled energies and human resources westwards and focused the nation upon a major national goal: settling and developing the West. It is possible that the Americans would see in Canada a modern counterpart of the West and the path of settlement would extend northward into the Mid-Canada Corridor and eventually into the Far North.

Going back to Canada's point of view, if free trade were to lead to a common market, without political integration, the country could increasingly become marginalized, possessing few effective powers of its own. The 'sovereignty-association' option, which free trade with the United States entails, must, therefore, be a transitionary option. It cannot last indefinitely as the 'sovereignty' part will become increasingly symbolic and the 'association' part increasingly real. Free trade is, therefore, an accelerator to higher forms of union, although the timing of the last political step may be longer than a few years. It may take a generation.

One possible determining factor is what happens to Europe after 1992. Already, since 1988, Europeans carry the same passport with European Community in large letters and 'France', 'Britain' or 'Belgium' in smaller ones. Will the symbolism become fact in the nineties? If the post-1992 European Community becomes a political entity, strong forces will induce Canada to do likewise with the United States. In addition, of course, if Southeast Asia moves forward and unites in an economic partnership of Japan, China and the four 'Mini-Dragons' (Hong Kong, South Korea, Singapore and Taiwan), the pressures on North America will become intolerable. Continental union will then be the logical solution.

Scenario 4 : Canadian Renaissance.

If not 'muddling through' or accepting a 'continental destiny' or Quebec separation, what then? What is the practical alternative and is it viable? In this author's view, the alternative is both practical and viable. If there is a will, there is a way. But is there a will? The answer is by no means self-evident. Under what conditions might a strong political will surface to lead Canada into rebuilding itself, thus maintaining its independence indefinitely? Significant progress would have to be made on the three fronts that constitute the building blocks of the 'Canadian Renaissance' scenario:

(1) A clear, national purpose, encased in a consensual mission statement;

(2) The creation of a new centrality in Canada that is not

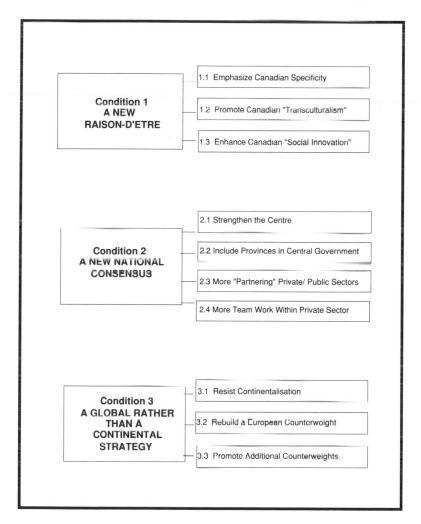

Figure 6
The Conditions for a Canadian Renaissance

adversarial but co-operative; and
(3) The maintenance of a diversified structure of external relations.

Condition 1:   A New Raison-d'être

The definition of a clear national purpose is an essential condition for a viable nation with the external threats Canada is facing.

As we discussed previously, this purpose need not be expressed in grandiloquent clichés, but should be persuasive enough to raise adrenalin levels and make Canadians excited about their country.

The building blocks of such a national purpose are basically three:

First, Canada's specificity must be emphasized. This is a variation of the historical 'other-than-America' theme, not in hostile fashion, but in what is called 'product-differentiation' in business circles.   If we do not differentiate our product we have nothing to offer.   In this sense, we must also get rid of the unconscious inferiority complex which tends to favour what is imported and what is not invented here as being clearly superior to local products.   This inferiority complex manifests itself, not only with respect to the United States but also, and perhaps more so, vis-à-vis Europe.   There is no objective reason to feel inferior at all.

Second, the national purpose must be built on the new syntheses that can come out of transculturalism.   We must use our diverse component cultures as elements to be combined into new mixtures, not as medieval castles to be surrounded by defensive moats.   This clearly favours a policy aimed at increasing communication and interchange between ethnic groups and providing incentives for new syntheses.   In addition, it argues in favour of a policy of nurturing new ideas and new entrepreneurs, who will emanate from that intercultural inter-paradigmatic dialogue.

Third, Canada's specificity should be developed along various themes of social innovation: new ways of doing things, experimenting with advanced concepts, dealing with old problems in dynamic and imaginative ways. Among the candidate areas for social innovation are:

(a) Rethinking the role of the state in the light of the new realities of the last decade of the twentieth century; arriving at an optimal role for the 'Leviathan' - not maximal and heavy-handed, but not superficially minimal and anaemic either;

(b) Giving a human face to high technology so that the scientific and technological culture that we will live in will not be dominated by inhuman machines but, instead, will be at the service of human self-fulfilment;

(c) Devising new ways of maintaining and enhancing mental and physical health and welfare;

(d) Promoting ecological development where human endeavours are much more in harmony with the environment.

Condition 2: A New National Consensus

In chess you can only win if you have a strong centre. Weaken your centre and the game is lost. In a federal state, whose only neighbour is the United States, if there is no strong centre then, as surely as in chess, the game will be lost. This has nothing to do with ideology. It has much to do with geopolitics, power relations, gravitational attraction and centrifugal forces. Recognizing this fact, Canada has, in the past, earnestly attempted to strengthen the centre but with very limited success. There is one fundamental reason for this: the Canadian centre, held by the federal government without the provinces, exacerbated adversarial relations. It was

exclusive rather than inclusive. It was a forum for conflict.
If there is to be a new centrality, it must be co-operative
and thrive on goal-congruence between the players. The
old zero-sum centrality, leading into 'auction' models,
where demands are escalated and every one tugs at the
centre, cannot work. To ensure a new centrality at least
three sub-conditions would have to be met:

First, the future central government should include
the provinces. As was indicated elsewhere, Canada is one
of the few federations where the provincial or state level of
government is not represented at the federal level. To
achieve this representation at least two methods may be
envisioned: a *House of the Provinces* replacing the
current Canadian Senate (an obvious proposal whose logic
is self-evident), and the designation of a *National
Priorities "Super-Cabinet"* which could be composed of
the ten provincial premiers, chaired by the national prime
minister. The "House of the Provinces" would allow the
provinces to be represented in the legislative branch. This
House should possess real powers, more akin to those of
the U.S. Senate, which is a "House of the States", rather
than to the present Canadian Senate, which is really a
replica of the British House of Lords - a wielder of
symbolic, not real, power.

The "National Priorities Super-Cabinet" would set
the strategic course for the nation. Once approved by the
combined Houses of Parliament, including the House of
the Provinces, this strategy should become the law of the
land, with no appeal possible. It would also be important
to build into this Super-Cabinet, decision-making rules that
do not require unanimity on all issues. Depending on the
nature of the issues, varying majorities could be required.
For some minor issues, a simple majority would be all that

would be needed. For medium-scope issues, stricter majorities, such as two-thirds or three-quarters, might be required. Finally, for life-and-death issues, unanimous consent might be needed. What constitutes a majority might be the subject of fine tuning. Majorities could be calculated with each of the ten provinces casting one vote and the federal prime minster casting the deciding vote, in case of a tie. Or, in some cases, a population-weighted majority might be conceived, to avoid the situation where very small Prince Edward Island might cancel Ontario or Quebec's vote. But whatever internal decision-making tools are chosen, this Super-Cabinet should not be vulnerable to second guessing or 'notwithstanding' clauses.

Would Quebec go for such a deal? At first glace, one would be tempted to answer "no". Why would Quebec cede power to a central body where, on some issues, it would not hold a veto and could be outvoted by the others. The current axiom in Quebec nationalist circles is that anything that weakens Canada, and especially Ontario, is good for Quebec. Conversely then, anything that strengthens Canada must be bad for Quebec. We believe that this 'axiom' is based on a strategic fallacy.

Assume, for purposes of argument, that we are all Quebec nationalists and that our principal, perhaps even our only, goal is to preserve the French language, way of life and culture of Quebec. At first glance, 'sovereignty' might appear to be the best way to achieve it. However, on closer analysis, it will become clear that sovereignty in the form of Quebec separation is *not* the best way to preserve the French language and culture. The reason is purely geopolitical. Quebec separation will accelerate the rest-of-Canada's continentalization and will drive the other provinces into the arms of the United States. Without

Quebec, the long-term probability of Canada surviving as a nation is very low. This is not because the rest of the country is weak, but rather because the U.S. alternative will become too attractive.

The immediate effect of Quebec separation might be, temporarily, to strengthen the rest-of-Canada's resolve to become united. However, centrifugal forces will continue to exist and the Maritimes will be cut off from the rest of the country. Linkages with the New England states are bound to increase with free trade. Newfoundland, having considered in the past joining the United States, will try to do so again and will be followed along that route by the other Atlantic Provinces. For different reasons, British Columbia, at the other extremity of the land, will be drawn into the California orbit. The Prairies, especially Alberta, perhaps the most pro-American of Canadian provinces, will not hesitate long before following suit. Ontario will be the last hold-out, since it is the province which benefits most from Confederation. Ultimately, however, it too will follow suit.

If that happens, what would be the long-term prospects of an independent Quebec, now surrounded by a 270 million-strong United States? In that situation, three options would be possible for Quebec - the 'Louisiana' route, the 'Puerto Rico' route or a new Euro-Option, now at the level of Quebec only, rather than Canada.

The Louisiana route involves merging with the United States, developing economically but, in the process, sacrificing a culture that will become more the subject of tourist attractions than a genuine way of life. Old Montreal will compete with the Latin Quarter in New Orleans, but, in the Louisiana option, voluntary assimilation is the long-term prospect. The Puerto Rico option involves a special status, a strong defence of the culture, but at the expense of an inevitable marginalization. The new Euro-option involves reviving the European connection and attempting to achieve, at the Quebec level, what has been tried, in the last two hundred years, at the Canadian level. The prospects for a Quebec/Europe axis are not, at present, strong and this scenario, at this stage, seems unlikely.

However, in this author's view, it is the only realistic option for Quebec independence, if that independence is desired. All other independence options for Quebec lead to an inevitable continental destiny (Louisiana) or high marginalization (Puerto Rico).

By a process of elimination, because of the geopolitical forces in play, *Quebec needs Canada as a buffer state vis-à-vis the United States.* Quebec wields, within Canada, much more influence than its sheer numbers warrant, because the rest of Canada, especially Ontario, has accepted to pay a high price for continued Quebec membership in Confederation

For instance, because Quebec tends to vote as a bloc in federal elections, Quebec tends to decide the outcome of those elections. Throughout the century, with a few notable exceptions, carrying Quebec has been the preferred way of becoming Prime Minister of Canada. In fact, for all of the twenty-four years, from 1968 to 1992, barring unforeseen circumstances, Canada's Prime Minister will have been a Quebecer, with the exception of the short-lived governments of Joe Clark, in 1979-80, and John Turner, in 1984. If the next leader of the Liberal Party is a Quebecer, this situation is likely to continue well into the nineties.

Within Canada, Quebec is strong. *Within an American Continent, Quebec will probably be much weaker and will have fewer bargaining 'chips'.* The strategic error that Quebec nationalists are committing is to over-estimate the rest-of-Canada's resilience and political will to remain separate from the United States after the departure of Quebec. This is because Quebec, mistakenly, confuses Ontario with the rest of Canada and believes that what is true for Ontario will hold for the rest of the country. In other words, the Quebec perception of Canada grossly under-estimates the centrifugal forces outside Quebec, such as Western separatism and Maritime discontent. If Quebec were more aware of the fragility of the rest of the country, after its possible departure, and of the likelihood of Canada's ultimate merger with the United States, it would think twice before weakening the centre.

The trick, then, for any future Prime Minister of Canada who would want to strengthen the centre *is to show that Quebec nationalism needs Canadian nationalism.* These two superficially opposing forces are objective allies. Canada's nationalism is weak and Quebec's is strong, but this is because Quebec has more to lose from the disintegration of Canada than the English provinces, with the exception of Ontario.

Again, we are talking geopolitics and objective alliances; we are not introducing ideology. Even if Quebec nationalists hated the Canadian version, they should back it for purely selfish reasons. In fact, the first order of business of an independent Quebec should be to provide cultural aid for English Canada to induce it to remain separate from the United States! As is often the case, there is a very human temptation to focus on immediate visible threats and ignore longer-term invisible ones - Louis XV famous syndrome, *après moi le déluge.* Superficial analysis yields superficial strategies. The superficial analysis is that by weakening Canada, Quebec becomes stronger. This may have been true in other times and other circumstances. But given the array of forces lined-up to dominate the nineties, this approach could end-up being a fatal strategic error. If this can be demonstrated to the satisfaction of Quebec nationalists, then the prospect of a new co-operative and inclusive centrality to lead Canada towards excellence will become possible.

If the New Centrality deals with the federal/ provincial, Quebec vs Canada adversarial systems, the other systems remain to be revamped. As was argued in Chapter 6, the Leviathan that is government, whether federal or provincial, must be rethought, without being castrated. Government activities were allowed to expand uncontrollably in the 1970s; the crude attempts that have been made to reverse the process have never fully understood the operative mechanisms. From the 'maximum' state of the seventies, complete with inflation, deficits, debt and the 'British disease' came the state-minimization policies of the eighties, spending cuts, taxation reform, privatization, deregulation, apparent abandonment of industrial strategy and lip-service paid to the virtues of free trade. This sudden transformation of the state from 'Santa Claus' to 'miserly stepmother' will, if pursued, have traumatic effects.

The principal challenge that is emerging for governments in the nineties will be to co-manage growing social complexity. The rapid technological change from which the growing complexity arises is creating short-term winners and losers, although the long-term potential is clearly of the 'win/win' variety.

The management of complexity will require better government participation in economic and social life.

However, although the responsibilities of government will not decrease, the ability to finance them through taxation will. In order to replace taxation as the principal source of government funding, new models of the state have to be explored. At this stage, the debate is too polarized between 'right' and 'left' when, in fact, both these concepts are becoming less and less relevant. Japan, the most successful capitalist economy, is also the most statist, but its statism is subtle and indirect, not heavy-handed and demotivating. The United States espouses the least statist philosophy, yet its enormous deficits and procurement policies are exactly equivalent to a more overt industrial policy.

In exploring new paradigms to allow the state to co-manage complexity with the private sector, certain key issues have to be tackled. Three basic ideas can become building blocks of a new theory of the state.

The first is the notion of a *productive public sector,* that will accept the discipline of the bottom line and be geared towards producing surpluses rather than deficits, without sacrificing the acquired rights brought in by the welfare state. This productive public sector could still produce essential services for all at no user-cost. Thus, the principle of universality could be retained. However, the delivery of these services would be subject to better rules of efficiency and the built-in incentives for waste would be removed.

In addition, the public sector would have to (a) supplement its dwindling taxation income and (b) absorb part of a redundant work force displaced by labour-saving technological progress. To do this, it would involve itself in lucrative productive activities to be sold on the open market.

Thus, although the 'dog' Crown corporations would be privatized, the 'milk cows' would be retained, and possibly added-to by acquisitions from the private sector. 'Privatization' would be supplemented by 'publicization', a symmetrical process to divide, more effectively, the labour between the two sectors. The intended rate of profit from the 'milk cows' would remain reasonable. There would be no attempt to maximize profits at the expense of the consumer or, alternatively, to run deficit operations at the expense of the taxpayer. Whatever deficits and debt exist, today, would be absorbed the natural way. *New income would reduce past deficits,* which is exactly what an individual or corporation does when they are in trouble. A thriving and productive public sector, not dependent on punitive taxation for its livelihood, would usher in a new concept of government.

If the state is going, in part, to think like a private corporation, it would be advisable *for private corporations to think, on occasion, like public bodies .* The more this is so, the less the state will be needed. Ultimately, the minimum state might be achieved by maximally, socially responsible citizens and corporations.

Social responsibility implies a sensitivity to externalities beyond the internal logic of profit maximization. This is the second feature of the new model that should be explored. In particular, in the employment field, successful corporations would have to resist the temptation to lay-off workers. Alternatively, if the dictates of competition force them to do so, the state will have to assume responsibility and provide jobs, or incomes, or both for these displaced workers.

The third, and most important, principle that should inspire future governments is the establishment of a partnership with the private sector. The partnership could take the form of joint ventures and, in particular, should develop the State-as-Coach idea - a low-profile state creating the conditions for maximum performance from the private sector. The modalities of such a model and its ramifications in terms of a national development strategy are complex, indeed, and cannot be fully explored here. Suffice it to say that between 'night watchman' on the one hand and 'God the Father' on the other, there are many intermediate models for the state to choose. Each model will have to be adapted to the cultural reality of the milieu and must be flexible. This much is certain, however: in the face of contemporary turbulence, neither Leviathan nor Lilliput as models for the state present any lasting chance of success.

In the search for New Centrality, due consideration must be given, at the level of labour/management relations, to what we have called the 'uncoupling hypothesis' - namely that productivity gains and economic growth no longer automatically mean more jobs and that, conversely, job creation may no longer lead automatically to wealth creation.

This 'uncoupling phenomenon', created by technological progress, not just in the last twenty years but over the last two hundred, is reaching an important new threshold as a result of the development of information technology. Robotics, bureautics, CAD (computer-assisted design), CAM (computer-assisted manufacturing), CAT (computer-assisted teaching) and, ultimately, CAE (computer-assisted everything!) is transforming the way we do things.

In order for all to profit from this phenomenon, tripartite joint planning bylLabour, management and

government is needed. Once more, the partnership will
yield much more than confrontation.

Finally, the New Centrality means that, at the level
of private sector industrial organization, certain 'sacred
cows' will have to be fundamentally reviewed, especially
concerning the optimum size of the firm. Small firms
produce more jobs than larger firms, and very small firms
produce the most jobs. However jobs and wealth creation
are now uncoupled. Very small firms have no staying
power and tend to be swept-away under pressure. At the
same time, enormous firms lose their innovative potential
and become dinosaurs.   Somewhere along the continuum
is the optimum-size firm - one that can benefit from
economies of scale, innovate freely and command
meaningful distribution channels to counter foreign
multinationals. If this optimum size is to be achieved,
competition laws will have to be reviewed, areas will have
to be targeted for concerted action, and competitiveness
transposed from the local to the international field.
Partnering, strategic alliances and consortia will have to
replace quaint, old-style individual competition.

Condition 3: A Global rather than a Continental Strategy

The third condition for a Canadian renaissance in
the nineties is the diversification of external relations in
order to avoid excessive continentalization of the Canadian
economy. Even with a strong national purpose and no
adversarial relations, Canada still needs an external
counterweight to the United States. Which country or
group of countries could provide this?

A Japanese counterweight might, at first sight, be
appealing. After all, we are talking about the rising world
superpower facing Canada across the Pacific. It could be
argued that what Europe gave to Canada in the nineteenth

century, Japan could give Canada in the twenty-first. Japan is, indeed, a great nation and much of this book has stressed its major strengths and how it could be an example for others, including Canada. That being said, a major Japanese connection for Canada, to the exclusion of others, appears somewhat dangerous.

Canada is, at present, ill-equipped to enter into an exclusive partnership with Japan. Institutionally weak, Canada could become the junior partner in such a duo - even more so than with the United States. On the purely economic plane, Japan is much more interested in the United States than in Canada. Its interest in Canada is principally-centred around natural resources.

A Japanese option might, therefore, mean that Canadians would continue playing the role of 'hewers of wood and drawers of water' for Japan, instead of for Europe and the United States. Japanese-owned factories might locate in Canada, in order to serve the United States market. However, they would only do so if Canada's competitive advantage, over possible alternative locations in the United States, were crystal clear - something that is by no means evident.

Secondly, politically and culturally there are not enough commonalities between the Japanese and Canadian experiences to allow the close cultural co-operation that Canada and Europe have enjoyed in the last two centuries. A sole Japanese counterweight to the United States in North America sounds, on the whole, somewhat far-fetched.

Latin America, and in particular Mexico, might be envisioned as a plausible counterweight, but it is not clear what the common interests of this bloc and Canada really are - other than fear of the United States. Besides,

Mexico is too weak and beset with too many internal problems to be able significantly to help Canada.

The 'Rest of the World' has been advanced, by some, as an appropriate counterweight. Under this scenario, Canada would diversify its trading relationships and reduce the volume of bilateral trade with the United States. It would rely on multilateral tariff reduction through the GATT Accords. On the political and cultural fronts, Canada would be active in global affinity groups, such as the Commonwealth and "La Francophonie". At the same time, the Canadian International Development Agency (CIDA), the International Development Research Centre (IDRC) and private firms would increase Canada's presence in the Third World. To some extent this 'Rest of the World' policy package is already present today and was, in fact, initiated as far back as the Pearson years. But can it resolve the geopolitical imbalance on this continent? Not very likely.

By a process of elimination, if there is to be a new credible external counterweight it would have to be either the old one, Europe, or a new one, with Canada as a central point in a triangular relationship involving the United States, Europe and Japan. The conditions for a closer Canada-Europe relationship, to develop beyond the signature of treaties and the holding of diplomatic cocktail parties, are as follows.

First, there must be a political will on both sides of the Atlantic. Such a will is not present now, but could possibly be developed in the future. In particular, the Central and Eastern provinces, Ontario, Quebec and the Maritimes on the Canadian side, continue to be interested in Europe. On the European side, the EEC would have to perceive Canada as a separate entity and not as a subset of the United States. In addition, national European governments would have to intensify their bilateral links with Canada.

Second, the European integration process would have to cross new thresholds. Once again, we come to the conclusion that a unified outward-looking Europe would be very attractive for Canada; on the other hand, a unified inward-looking Europe or a Europe disunited, whether inward or outward looking, would be much less attractive. If the United States of Europe become a political reality, by the end of the century, Canada's links with the old Continent could become extremely valuable.

The other variant of the revised counterweight scenario would make Canada a major 'go-between' with Europe, Japan and the United States. Here, Canada could make good use of its transcultural skills. It would act as middleman between the Europeans, the Japanese and the Americans - a most natural role given Canada's heritage and history. If economic conditions were appropriate, then European and Japanese industry and investment capital would locate in Canada, in order to serve the U.S. market. This 'triangular option' would be feasible under certain circumstances. It would, nevertheless, require enough independence on the part of the Canadian governments to create the appropriate attractive conditions.

The Bottom Line

When all is said and done, what lies ahead in the nineties? Four scenarios have been presented as major historical thrusts. Of course, scenario-building can be extended into a useful simulation game and dozens of additional scenarios concocted. However, whether the ultimate number is four or four hundred, the basic underlying issues remain the same. The status quo, with its unclear directions and ambivalence, is setting Canada in a cancellation mode. To reverse this slow 'meltdown', clear directions are needed: Continental Destiny, Quebec Separation or a Canadian Renaissance. The status quo cannot survive, in our view, beyond the nineties and has to be replaced by one of the other three. The Quebec independence scenario is, in our analysis, an intermediate not a final stage, since most paths lead from it back to Continental Destiny. In other words, the long-term perspective yields not an *embarras du choix* but a dichotomy. Rebuilding the nation, or cancelling it - not by speeches from the Throne, but by letting natural forces unfold.

It is important to stress, however, that all four scenarios depict varying degrees of success for Canada, from the bronze to the gold. On these grounds, the prognosis must be deemed good to excellent.

Canada remains amongst the luckiest nations on earth. Its problems, immense as they may seem to the internal observer, are minor irritations in the scale of human suffering. Whereas African populations are struggling to ensure their physical survival and escape famine, whereas certain Asian and Latin American countries live under the sword of Damocles, threatened by neighbours or internal civil wars, whereas parts of Europe are struggling with de-industrialization and overcrowding, Canada's problems are considerably less intense.

Canada has to choose between the middling and the superlative. In the worst case, it will continue 'muddling through' for a while and eventually choose a direction. In the 'muddling through' phase it will forego excellence, but most certainly stay in the first heat. Barring a major ecological disaster, a nuclear war or an uncontrolled epidemic - scenarios which are likely to hit any country and are not reserved for Canada alone - the outlook is favourable and optimism is justified.

However, for those who want more, for those who are not content with bronze, for those who believe life is extending oneself to the maximum of one's ability, rather than idling along with the gentleman's 'C', present and past performance must be judged unsatisfactory and unworthy of a country so well-favoured by nature and circumstance.

We can do much better. But we are not likely to do much better, in the present adversarial mode, where the cancellation of initiative seems to be the rule of the day, when 'shilly-shallying' and having the knack for choosing bad compromises seem prominent national traits. As the Bard said, "Men at some time are sometimes masters of their fate. The fault, dear Brutus, lies not in our stars but in ourselves that we are underlings ..."

SELECT BIBLIOGRAPHY

Aubin, François. *René Levesque tel quel.* Montréal: Les Editions Boréal Express, 1973.

Atkinson, A.B. and J.S. Fleming. *Lectures on Public Economics.* New York: Mc Graw Hill, 1980.

Barbé, Jean Michel. *Les Chômeurs du Québec.* Ottawa: Editions Parti pris, 1977.

Beck, Stanley M. et al. eds. *Canada and The New Constitution: The Unfinished Agenda.* Ottawa: Tri-Graphic Printing Ltd., 1983.

Beck, M. "The Expanding Public Sector: Some Contrary Evidence". *National Tax Journal* March 1976.

—-. *Government Spending, Trends and Issues.* New York: Praeger, 1981.

Bergeron, Gérard. *L'Indépendance: oui, mais ... .* Montréal: Les Editions Quinze, 1977.

Bernard, André. *What does Quebec want?* Toronto: James Lorimer & Company, 1978.

—-. *Québec: Elections 1976.* Montréal: Editions Hurtubise HMH, 1976.

Bouchette, Errol. *L'Indépendance économique du Canada français.* Montréal: Les Editions La Presse, 1977.

Bourassa, Robert. *Deux fois la Baie James.* Montréal: Les Editions La Presse, 1981.

Breton, Raymond, Jeffrey G. Reitz, and Victor Valentine. *Cultural Boundaries and the Cohesion of Canada.* Montréal: The Institute for Research on Public Policy, 1980.

Breton, Raymond. *The Canadian Condition.* Montréal: Institute for Research on Public Policy, 1977.

Broadway, R., and H. Kitchen. *Canadian Tax Policy.* 2nd ed. Toronto: Canadian Tax Foundation, 1984.

Brossard, Jacques. *L'Accession à la souveraineté et le cas du Québec.* Montréal: Presses de l'Université de Montréal, 1976.

Byers, R.B. et al. ed. *Canada Challenged: The Viability of Confederation.* Toronto: Bryan Press Ltd., 1979.

Cameron, Duncan et al. ed. *The Other MacDonald Report.* Toronto: James Lorimer & Company, 1985.

—-. "The Expansion of the Public Economy: A Comparative Analysis". *American Political Review* December 1978.

Carmichael, Edward A. *Reorienting the Canadian Economy.* Toronto: C.D. Howe Institute, 1985.

Clement, Wallace. *The Canadian Corporate Elite.* Toronto: McClelland and Stewart Limited, 1975.

Clift, Dominique. *Quebec Nationalism in Crisis*.
Montréal: McGill-Queens University Press, 1982.

Cohen, Dian, and Kristin Shannon. *The Next Canadian
Economy*. Montréal: Eden Press, 1984.

Cornwall, John, and Wendy Maclean. *Economic Recovery
for Canada*. Ottawa: Canadian Institute for Economic
Policy, 1984.

Dauphin, Roma. *Les options économiques du Québec*.
Montréal: Editions du Jour, 1971.

Deblock, Christian and Richard Arteau. *La politique
économique canadienne à l'épreuve du continentalisme*.
Montréal: GRETSE/ACFAS, 1988.

Desbarats, Peter. *Canada lost, Canada found: The Search
for a New Nation*. Toronto: McClelland and Stewart, 1981.

Dion, Léon. *Le Québec et le Canada, les voies de l'avenir*.
Montréal: Les Editions Québécois, 1980.

Drache, Arthur. *B.C., The Great Tax Rip-off*. Toronto:
McClelland and Stewart Ltd., 1982.

Dupont, Pierre. *15 novembre 1976*. Montréal: Les Editions
Quinze, 1976.

Foulon A. and G. Hatchuel. "The Redistribution of Public
Funds in France in 1965 and 1970". *Review of Income
and Wealth* September 1978.

Fournier, Louis. *F.L.Q: Histoire d' un mouvement clandestin.* Montréal: Editions Québec/Amerique, 1982.

Fournier, Pierre. *The Quebec Establishment.* Montréal: Black Rose Books Ltd., 1976.

Friedman, Milton. *Friedman on Galbraith.* Toronto: Fraser Institute, 1977.

Gamma Institute. *Values and The Conserver Society.* Montréal: Université de Montréal/McGill Press, 1976.

Gollner Andrew and Salée Daniel, eds. *Canada Under Mulroney.* Montréal: Véhicule Press, 1988.

Grant George. *Lament for a Nation.* Princeton, N.J.: Van Nostrand, 1965.

Grubel, H.G. and M.A. Walker. *Unemployment Insurance: Global Evidence of its Effect on Unemployment.* Vancouver: The Fraser Institute, 1978.

Gwyn, Richard. *The 49th Paradox.* Toronto: McLelland and Stewart, 1985.

Harbron, John D. *Canada without Quebec.* Toronto: Musson Book Company, 1977.

Jenkin, Michael. *The Challenge of Diversity.* Ottawa: Minister of Supply and Services, 1983.

Kierans, Tom. *Remixing the Economy*. Toronto: The Institute for Research on Public Policy, 1985.

Latouche, Daniel. *Premier Mandat - Une prospective à court terme du gouvernement Pequiste.*

Tome I *L'Economie/Le Social.* Montréal: Les Editions de l'Aurore, 1977.

TomeII, *Le Culturel/Le Politique.* Montréal: Les Editions de l'Aurore, 1977.

Laxer, James, et al. *Le Canada des Libéraux - Pierre Elliot Trudeau et sa survivance de la confédération.* Toronto: James Lorimer Company, 1977.

Lazae, Fred. *The New Protectionism - Non Tariff Barriers and Their Effects on Canada.* Toronto: James Lorimer & Company, 1981.

Lévesque, René. *Option Québec.* Montréal: Editions de l'Homme, 1968.

Meekison, Peter J. *Canadian Federation: Myth or Reality?* New York: Methuen Publications, 1977.

Milner, Henry, et al. *The Decolonization of Quebec - An Analysis of Left Wing Nationalism.* Toronto: McClelland & Stewart, 1973.

Minford, P. *Unemployment: Causes and Cure.* Oxford: Martin Robertson, 1983.

Monnet, François-Marie. *Le défi Québécois.* Montréal:
Editions Quinze, 1977.

Montmarquette, Claude, ed. *Economie du Québec et choix
politiques.* Montréal: Les Presses de l'Université du
Québec, 1975.

Morton, W.L. *The Canadian Identity.* 2nd ed. Madison:
University of Wisconsin Press, 1972.

Murray, Vera. *Le parti Québécois: de la fondation à la
prise du pouvoir.* Montréal: Hurtubise Editions HMH,
1976.

Newman, Peter C. *The Canadian Establishment.* Toronto:
McClelland and Stewart, Bantam, 1975.

Nicol, Eric, and Peter Whalley. *Canada Cancelled Because
of Lack of Interest.* Edmonton: Hurtig, 1977.

Niosi, Jorge. *Le contrôle financier du capitalisme
canadien.* Montréal: Presses de l'Université du Québec,
1978.

OECD. *Tax Expenditures: A Review of Issues and Country
Practices.* Paris, 1984.

Orban, Edmond. *Un modèle de souveraineté-association?*
Le Conseil Nordique. Montréal: Editions Hurtubise HMH
Ltée, 1978.

Palda, Kristian S. *Industrial Innovation.* Vancouver: The
Fraser Institute, 1984.

Patry, André. *Le Québec dans le monde*. Ottawa: Les Editions Lémeac Inc., 1980.

Pryor, F.L. *Public Expenditures in Communist and Capitalist Nations*. London: George Allen and Unwin, 1968.

Reynolds, M. and E. Smolensky. *Public Expenditures and the Distribution of Income*. New York: Academic Press, 1977.

Robert, Jean-Claude. *Du Canada français au Québec libre - histoire d'un mouvement indépendantiste*. Paris: Flammarion, 1975.

Rohmer, Richard. *Separation*. Toronto: McClelland and Stewart, 1976.

Rotstein, Abraham. *Rebuilding from Within - Remedies for Canada's Ailing Economy*. Toronto: James Lorimer & Company, 1981.

Royal Commission On the Economic Union of Canada. *The Macdonald Commission Report*. Ottawa: 1985.

Ryan, Claude, ed. *Le Québec qui se fait*. Montréal: Hurtubise HMH, 1971.

—-*Une société stable*. Montréal: Les Editions Héritage, 1978.
Sandmo, A. "Optimal Taxation - An Introduction to the Literature" *Journal of Public Economics* July-August, 1976.

Saunders Peter and Friedrich Klau. *The Role of the Public Sector*. OECD Economic Studies, Special Issue, Spring 1985.

Séguin, Maurice. *L'idée d'idépendance au Québec*. Montréal: Le Boréal Express Ltée, 1977.

Stacy, Richard. *Canadian Real Estate*. Toronto: Peter Martin Associates Ltd, 1968.

Tellier, Luc-Normand, ed. *Qui décide au Québec?* Montréal: Les Editions Quinze, 1978.

The Economist, Intelligence Unit. *The World in 1987*.

Thorburn, H.G. *Planning and the Economy Building Federal/Provincial Status*. Toronto: James Lorimer & Company, 1984.

Toffler, Alvin. *The Third Wave*. New York: Bantam Books, 1980.

Tremblay, Rodrique. *Indépendance et marché commun*. Ottawa: Editions du Jour, 1970.

Tremblay, Rodrique. *Le Québec en crise*. Montréal: Presses Sélect Ltée, 1981.

Trudeau, Pierre Elliot. *Federalism and the French Canadians*. Toronto: Macmillan of Canada, 1968.

Valaskakis, Kimon. *Le Québec et son destin international - Les enjeux géopolitiques*. Montréal: Les Editions Quinze, 1980.

Valaskakis, Kimon, Peter S. Sindell, Graham J. Smith, and Iris Fitzpatrick-Martin. *The Conserver Society*. New York: Harper & Row, 1979.

Vallières, Pierre. *Un Québec impossible*. Ottawa: Editions Québec/l'Amérique, 1977.

Vellas, Pierre. *Canada 1987-88*. Paris: Economica, 1988.

Wade, Mason. *The French Canadians: 1760 - 1967*. Toronto: Macmillan Company of Canada Ltd, 1968.

Walker, Michael. *Focus on Flat-Rate Tax Proposals*. Vancouver: The Fraser Institute, 1983.

NOTES

NOTES

NOTES